Quality

by Design

Quality by Design

@2022 Craig Risi

ISBN: 978-0-6397-0368-8

Acknowledgments

I would like to take the time to thank all those who have helped me on my software development and testing journey. There are too many to mention here, but almost every person I've had the privilege of working with has had an impact in some way in shaping my thoughts around software quality, testing, and the importance of good design.

I have learned so much from many people and even the many thoughts I share in this book, are based on experiences I have gained directly and indirectly from all the amazing smart minds that have shaped my career.

Life is worth far more than our careers though which is why I want to devote this book most of all to my amazing wife, Jacqui Risi who has been my rock and support for almost 15 years and allowed me to thrive in my career. Without her continued love and support that she brings to my life, it's unlikely that I would've been in a position where I could thrive the way I did – so I would like to dedicate this book to her and thank her for allowing me to spend the many hours after work learning and trying to develop myself and follow my passions.

Here's to many more amazing years and adventures ahead.

Contents

Introduction

This has been a book many years in the making. I have been writing a software development blog for over 5 years and have been contemplating putting together a book on my different thoughts and experiences ever since then.

The problem though has never been a lack of ideas, inspiration, or topics, as my regular blog topics can testify to. Rather, the biggest challenge for me has always been in how I would go about structuring a book that deals with software quality and various aspects of testing. I didn't want to simply write another book on testing, because - as my book will show — that will defeat a lot of what I believe about developing software quality, which is that it is best developed from the beginning and requires effort from an entire team to make a reality. It's not just something that we should allow our testing team to think about.

At the same time, if I focus exclusively on software design and architecture, then there is a good chance that testers and managers may miss out on the book because it is too technical for them and then also miss out on some important information that it is critical, they understand too.

So, in the end, I have decided to start my efforts by writing a book on software quality that combines all basic elements of design, testing, and quality governance so that engineers of all types can better understand what it takes to build and design quality software.

My hope is this will allow more people to read and understand the process in its entirety and hopefully collaborate better together to achieve this aim. I will also look to perhaps expand on the separate topics of software design and testing in deeper ways through separate books that will cater to developers and testers more specifically. But even then, I would like a book like this to serve as the foundation upon which they can build upon and start their process to better quality design.

It's for this reason that I've also avoided trying to split the book into parts that separate testing and development – and while there are certain parts of that to help the book flow better – to rather allow readers to gain exposure to every topic that I look to discuss.

I also understand that software is constantly evolving and there are many different approaches that one can take to good software design – depending on the purpose and need of the software itself. So, even though I know not everything in this book may suit every organization, I hope that people can consider the core principles that I teach and see how they can best apply them to your problem space. I do endeavor though, to try and consider as many possible ways as possible and try not to go into too many specific details in this book, to ensure that it has as wide-reaching an impact as possible.

My hope with this book is that it helps all people involved in developing software to think a little differently about how they go about designing, building, and testing their respective software applications to deliver on the promise of better-quality software.

If you're someone who's not sure what quality means, then this book can help you to see just how important quality is for every company. Ensuring that software is built with intentionality to deliver lasting value to users, developers, and companies alike. I hope you enjoy this journey and look forward to seeing and learning how people apply some of these principles in the future.

The Importance of Quality

I have come across many books, articles, and blogs that all speak about various aspects of software testing, automation, and testable design. Too many to even attempt to list here such is the richness of the resources available on these topics to any aspiring or even experienced software developer or tester. At the same time, my career has led me to work on a variety of software projects of varying degrees of success, whether that be measured by the number of defects, customer satisfaction, or financial return on investment. All very important measures of good, functional business software.

And the one abundantly clear thing is that those applications which can deliver lasting value with very few defects, while remaining highly maintainable (an important aspect of software quality that is often missed) is that this quality can be determined very early on by the way it Is approached during its design phase.

The truth is, whether we like to admit it or not, quality software is not built in retrospect of good coding or testing practices, but by the design of the software itself. As you go through this book, I hope to show you aspects of how we can approach developing software differently that will help you develop software that can be determined as "high quality" (which I will define in more detail in the next chapter). Making your resulting software far more effective and satisfying to work with.

The Importance of Quality

At the same time, given that there remains an important testing aspect to building quality software, I will spend time on ways to approach software testing and help build the required testing frameworks that can also help to further these aims.

We will start by looking at quality at a high level. Trying to understand how the concept of software quality has changed over the years. Then set a broader definition of software quality, along with why we tend to fail at it so often. Before looking into solutions on how to design and test software correctly to solve these issues and getting into some of the more exciting technical details. I do this because an important part of improving anything is understanding the core of the problem and where it went wrong in the first place.

However, I do understand that very few people will probably have the opportunity to design software systems entirely from scratch in their careers. Often, we are assigned to projects which are attached to various software architectures that are quite well established or even considered "legacy" in nature. Brought into projects which are far along in development and therefore we have little chance of influence around its design or – even worse – given software that is poorly designed and stuck having to maintain and build testing around it to try and keep it operating at an acceptable functional level.

In all these cases, try and learn what you can to apply wherever possible. Making changes at even a process level can have a substantial impact on future software delivery and help to fix things on existing and future projects. As long as we make a concerted effort to address quality issues in our respective projects and teams, we can move forward and work towards designing and building better software.

The Evolution of Software Quality

As we start our journey into exploring how to build quality software, it's worth looking into how the art of software quality assurance and, by extension, software testing has evolved. Much like all aspects of software engineering and like any growing technology, the science of developing software has drastically changed over the years. And along with these advancements, so should the way we approach both the design and testing of software to ensure we can deliver high-quality software.

As you will learn in the next chapter, not only is the list of variables that has an impact on a system quite large and arguably growing but so too is the way we are approaching software design and development drastically changing. Not just in terms of new and emerging technologies like cloud, blockchain, or different operating systems and platforms. But specifically, the speed at which we develop software.

The importance of getting features or software updates from concept generation to production is drastically reducing. Thanks to a high level of competition between the big companies and the cut-throat start-up market, companies want to be able to deliver new features to customers before their competitors to be able to differentiate themselves in this market.

This has led to the creation of continuous delivery pipelines and an effort to push multiple releases to production a day in many large companies. A move that is a positive one with regards to risk mitigation, but also a dangerous one as it places an increasing number of opportunities for things to go wrong in the development chain.

Combine this with the increasing intolerance we have towards software that doesn't work as expected and you have the platform for design decisions that can lead to many mistakes.

Balancing the Quality Triangle

Typically, to produce quality in any engineering project even outside of software, you need to factor in three things: cost, scope, and time.

Cost represents the overall budget that will be spent on a project and in the software world, is largely based on the costs of people working on the project with a small subset also going towards tools and infrastructure.

Scope represents the size of the features and functionality that need to be delivered.

Time represents the amount of time that the above features would need to be delivered.

Essentially, to balance quality, you need to ensure that you keep these things in balance. Trying not to do too many things too quickly will cause quality issues or require a reduction in scope to get the features out by a certain deadline. At the same time, having too few people on a project (or too few people lacking sufficient expertise or experience) will also slow things down or cause missteps in the quality of the final solution.

So, with the need to deliver software quicker, there is a bigger emphasis placed on balancing the size of the team and the scope that is delivered to ensure quality can be maintained. This may not always be feasible, depending on what work needs to get done but is typically managed in a modern Agile and DevOps world by releasing smaller things more frequently.

In theory at least. Because the reality is many organizations struggle to do this effectively and the reason is because of the way they approached the design of their software process, they did not factor in how to do so effectively with quality as the result.

Quality is more than just software testing

The idea of software quality has transcended the expertise of software testing, with which it is often so closely associated.

And rather moved towards a combination of all software development efforts and the synergy in which they are integrated to work together. Quality cannot be assured through testing but through deliberate planning and effort.

Quality is also not just judged by how defect-free the software appears to be, but also through its maintainability, secureness, efficiency of use, and the ability for teams to work together to build and maintain it with as little waste as possible. It's about meeting the needs of its users, without creating unnecessary bottlenecks of manpower and process along the way. It is maximizing the potential of software to deliver its purpose as profitability and cost-effectively as possible.

Yes, quality is at the center of the software development process and indeed the companies who use it. Quality is something that you will read about in many companies' promises about how good their software is. And yet, somehow few understand what developing quality software actually means.

I wrote this book because I wanted to bring a different perspective on software quality. Most often the focus is on the practice of software testing and how through efficient testing you can assure the software of your quality.

The truth is though that designing software of high quality has little to do with testing or more to do with intelligent design. If you want to make high-quality software, it is the process of deliberate design of the software and less the excellence of the software testing conducted. This is not to mitigate the science of testing which remains an integral part of the process, but rather is just to highlight how important all prospects of software architecture, design, analysis, process, and, yes, testing, are required to work together to make software of high quality.

None of this is possible by just focusing on one aspect of software development but the whole. And by making a deliberate effort as software engineers to align all these together to allow for better quality. Quality is the outcome of proper software engineering principles and a deliberate effort. Yes, aspects of quality can be achieved through elements of these software engineering principles but are unlikely to be long-lasting or achieve maximum effectiveness without all these aspects coming together.

Similarly, the testing or quality engineering profession has had to evolve to become one that is increasingly technical and combines the skills of every facet of software development to ensure that quality aspects in terms can work with members from the other aspects of teams in an effective manner.

Defining Quality

The word "quality" can be rather subjective and probably means different things to each of us. To one it may mean that an application passes all its tests, to another, it may just mean that their code can simply be deployed. While to a business, it may be more a matter of customer and revenue impact that occurs when defects arise in production.

The thing is most often we think of trying to measure the quality of software by focusing on the defects that affect customers in our software system's released state. By thinking of quality merely from a defect perspective we are losing out on understanding the many areas which determine the usability of the software. And by having a broader view of what makes up "quality" software, you can better build software that is not just "free of bugs," but meets the needs of the customers, businesses and so many other areas.

And as such, there is no one definition of quality. Even if you look for one online, you will find many different takes on software meeting its various functional and non-functional requirements. But nothing that paints the full picture of what truly defines software quality.

Software quality can probably best be defined as software that achieves its purpose. However, what is that purpose? As its more than just meeting the initial requirements laid out by the business and needs to take into consideration the use and maintenance of a software product (even if it's not fully understood at the time of conception) and needs to tie into a company's revenue or growth stream. Or operate at an efficient cost if it's not revenue impacting.

So given the true broad scope of what software requirements truly are and how quality is tied into that broader definition, I will attempt to detail factors that should be considered and incorporated into our measurement of software quality. Not all software is the same or has an equal purpose. So, my intention in this chapter is not to provide a definitive answer, but rather to provide the attributes that constitute software quality. With the intention for teams and companies to then purpose fit these attributes into their context to shape what quality means to their organization.

What constitutes a software system?

Before that, I want to identify the elements that make up a software system. Even though we may be working on software projects with a finite scope that we are responsible for, no software system operates in isolation. And we can effectively measure the quality of software if we look at it from its entire system and not simply the code that was delivered.

Code under development

This is the code that is currently getting developed. When we are looking at any existing project, the aspect that will get the most attention is the code or new functionality/application that is getting created/modified, or fixed.

Code or applications that are integrated

Most code or applications won't operate in isolation but be part of a greater software environment – either developed in-house or via third-party providers – that also shape the operation of the software. And, as such, when we're thinking of software quality in a software system, we need to be thinking about the bigger connected operation of all parts. Not just the code we are intending to deliver.

Data

Software generally runs on data. Whether it's a variety of databases, a blockchain system, or a variety of other data stores. How data is utilized and stored in a system forms an important part of its operation and needs to be factored into our understanding of the software system

Host infrastructure

Code needs to run somewhere. Whether it be on physical servers or virtual machines sitting on different cloud providers. We need to think about the makeup of how these functions when thinking about how these aspects may impact our software.

Network

Software needs to speak to different components of the system or external users and all this works through a network. A network which is a combination of the internet, internal and third-party or cloud configurations that all need to talk to each other.

Understanding the different aspects of the network and how they will impact the software is vital. And this includes such things as Load Balancers and Firewall services which have a massive impact on the operation of the software.

Test and automation framework

We want to test our software and have automation in place for continuous delivery and regression purposes. However, much like testing is sometimes wrongly considered as a separate function from development, we make the same mistake with the test frameworks themselves.

Even if test frameworks never get deployed to production with the rest of the code, they have a significant impact on the overall quality of the delivered code, and we need to consider the design and operation of these tests as an important part of our software design.

Deployment Tooling

We make use of tooling to move our code from different test environments to eventually deploy it into production. This tooling, and the different jobs and steps that it follows to perform these tasks form part of our overall software solution and we need to consider their operation and impact when designing, building, and testing our software.

Monitoring

We need to know what is going on with our software when it is in operation either in a production environment or a test environment and monitoring provides us with that useful information – in a variety of different forms. All these different tools and processes are things we should consider as influencing our final software system.

Support Tooling

Sadly, software is not just a deploy and leave-alone thing. We need to maintain and support it for a variety of reasons from patches, and updates to just general maintenance. All the different tooling that enables this may not seem like an immediate part of your software system under consideration but considering the impact our software design and operation has on these aspects, it is something we need to consider.

People

And lastly, we have people. Software may be code but is built with humans and for humans in some way or another. Its operation and ease of use are all aspects of a software system that need to fall under consideration. Plus, we need to factor in the critical human cost in the development of it.

Attributes of software quality

Now that we understand all the parts that constitute our software system, we can look at the different factors that make up the determination of its quality.

Software needs to meet its known functional requirements

Getting the obvious one out of the way. Software needs to be first measured by whether it meets the functional requirements set out for it. This is the core business or usage reason behind what the software is intended to do and should preferably be detailed in how the software achieves this to ensure it meets this need correctly. (I discuss this topic further in chapter 4).

Software needs to meet non-functional requirements

Businesses might look at what the software functionally does, but there is a lot more to what is going on in the details of how the system works than what it does. In fact, the list of things that should form part of a system's non-functional requirements is quite large with some aspects detailed enough to warrant an item on their own in this list.

The list of non-functional requirements that should factor into the idea of quality in the software team include:

- **Usability** — How easy is it to use the product? What defines the experience of using the product? We don't just need to ensure our software performs the required task but can do so in a way that is intuitive to the end-user or consuming systems.
- **Security** — Security is a massive part of the software industry, and any software system needs to cater to a variety of different security measures. Including how it deals with data, and privacy and can withstand a variety of attacks and malicious software viruses. This is such a massive part of software design, that I will be devoting a few chapters to this non-functional aspect later.
- **Capacity** — Systems don't operate infinitely and so it's useful to understand the expectations of its usage and data requirements. What are your system's storage requirements, today and in the future? How

will your system scale up for increasing volume demands? The answers to these questions can have a big impact on how you approach the design of your system.

- **Compatibility** — As mentioned earlier in this chapter – software doesn't operate in isolation and needs to work with other systems. Both internally and externally. For instance, all web software needs to work with a variety of different browsers and hardware configurations and this needs to be accounted for in the final solution

- **Reliability and Availability** — Software needs to work and be available to users. Knowing the expectations of when those users will need to use the software factors into how we think about its design. And this goes beyond just ensuring that the software works correctly but is also reflected in the architectural design of the overall system.

- **Scalability** – Also often known as the Black Friday test, named after how retail sites need to be able to adapt to the increased loads faced during the annual Black Friday craze. This sounds similar to capacity but deals less with long-term system usage and focuses on a software system's ability to adjust to unusual usage. Questions to consider here in your design are things like what are the highest workloads under which the system will still perform as expected?

- **Load and Performance** — This is another very important non-functional requirement that will get its own chapter devoted to it. Ensuring that software is designed for the relevant load and can perform according to certain expectations is critical to its operation and how we need to approach its design.

- **Regulatory** — There are a variety of regulatory and compliance frameworks that software may need to meet depending on the industry they fall in and are there requirements you need to satisfy for compliance?
- **Environmental** — Global warming and reducing greenhouse emissions are important things. And while the power efficiency of our software system should matter to us, this goes beyond that and should also factor into the user environment that the software will be expected to perform in. Think about the difference between military or flight software which is critical in their operation and performance and reliability are far more important than pretty graphics versus a social media platform where this is incredibly important.

Software needs to make a measured ROI

This is only relevant for business software, but it is still a factor that many teams don't even think about. And that is because you could argue that the (Return on Investment) ROI on software features is not the realm of the software developers, but rather the business. But that doesn't mean that the engineering team shouldn't be working to factor these things in.

In achieving the core functional requirements, software should achieve its purpose and thereby meet the necessary return on investment. Much depends on the way the code is delivered that will determine this. Software that works poorly is either not going to be used or requires a lot of extra effort to fix – all hampering the expected ROI of the software.

Similarly, software that is difficult to maintain, build or test (more on these topics later) will lead to longer development times and have an impact on ROI.

So, while it may not seem like something that a software team is directly responsible for, the quality of a team's work has a big bearing on the overall success of how a software application helps to allow a company to be financially successful.

As teams, we need to understand the revenue criteria that may determine our software systems' success and ensure we design our systems to meet those criteria.

Software quality needs to reduce the support effort of a company

A common function of many companies is their ability to support and service their clients. Software should help to streamline this effort. While not all software might be intended for this, it still has an impact on the overall ability of an organization to provide support and service to clients.

Software that doesn't work as expected, leads to functionality breaking, makes users unhappy, and often increases the number of service requests (SR) that companies must handle.

When software works reliably, this SR Support greatly goes down. So, in a way, the quality of a software product has some bearing on a company's ability to support its core business function and we need to factor this into our understanding and definition of what truly represents software quality.

Software needs to be easy to maintain

There are many different rules and standards that can be put in place to ensure that code is structured and documented in a certain way to make it easier to maintain. The same goes for the make-up of its architecture and testing frameworks and whether they support easy updating, fixing, and testing of software or whether it will require significant amounts of rework.

Software needs to meet its intended lifespan

We may not always think about software having a shelf-life. After all, unlike manufactured goods, software can constantly be updated and upgraded to adapt to newer computing technologies.

However, this is a misconception. You can't simply upgrade an underlying server or patch yourself out of a problem. Technology may improve over time, but this often renders many aspects of our software stack obsolete over time, so we need to consider that our software needs to support a certain amount of change to ensure its smooth operation.

Understanding the intention for the functionality long-term will shape the way the software is architected and affects the way you approach the code design.

Quality touches every aspect of software design

Understanding that a software system in its entirety is incredibly vast and that quality impacts every aspect of it can be a daunting prospect. You wouldn't be wrong for thinking achieving real software quality is practically impossible to achieve, but thankfully there are a lot of things that we can do to set us up for designing software that can be considered high quality.

However, before we start looking at some tips that will help us achieve better quality design. We need to understand why so many companies and teams get it so fundamentally wrong.

Where Quality Fails

I believe that an important aspect of any improvement is the ability to learn from the past. In understanding the experiences of both our successes and failures – and those of others. And so, it is important in looking to look at the reasons why the implementation of successful quality design in the software engineering world is such a rarity. In the hope that we can endeavor to not pursue these same mistakes in our design efforts.

Quality failures occur not as the result of any one thing, but rather as a combination of aspects that do not align or attribute to excellent quality practice. It is often a multitude of things that can lead to the final product not fitting together.

When we release software that has a high number of defects, has poor performance, stability issues, or security vulnerabilities, we often rush to find out how we could've missed this during our development cycle and make plans to then spruce up their testing efforts or address immediate technical concerns. But few companies focus on changing their outlook on quality.

Quality is the result of a company culture
Culture and processes will often have an even bigger impact on quality than any testing effort can ever derive. If we only on just an aspect of testing without addressing these other areas, we will likely fail in adequately addressing the quality concerns within a team.

So, what exactly is a poor-quality culture and how can impact the design of your software?

Well, firstly, a poor-quality culture is one where the delivery of a team or company is more focused towards delivery, achieving a specific tech goal or simply making money. Now, these goals are not inherently wrong. However, when they are the main drivers of your design, many quality aspects can be pushed aside. Resulting in teams either caring little about the overall quality of the solution or trying to work around the problem with aggressive forms of testing Even though – as you will realize – this is counterintuitive to delivering quality.

Now many companies may say they are focused on software quality and take it seriously, but this is not something you can simply tack on later. To be quality-focused is to drive everything with quality in mind and build your software, processes, and even culture around it. Not something that is easy to do.

Building everything with quality in mind might sound like an obvious thing to do and most companies may even believe they have done it. The reality though is that many companies haven't fully grasped what quality means or how to build it, leaving them with a false sense of surety in believing all is well. Whereas the reality is there are many potential pitfalls that they may soon face or indeed are tackling already.

This doesn't mean that your company is necessarily riddled with production defects or poorly performant. However, what it could mean is that there may be issues at scale or in the maintainability of both your software and your teams that are likely to grow over time because you have not taken the right quality approach. Functionality is important but the maintainability and scalability of the software may have an even bigger impact as the usage evolves and the surrounding software evolves. Software is constantly evolving and changing, and you need to design your systems to still deliver on quality despite change and even be able to adapt to it as much as possible.

While quality is the most critical aspect of getting quality right, there are more specific things in how it may impact software that we need to highlight.

The truth is that it's any one thing and the absence of just one thing can cause quality to break down. I will try and provide some simplification of the things that can cause quality in a company to fail and if you're struggling with quality in your organization, it might be worthwhile looking at these things and collectively changing them.

1) The software is built around the wrong architecture
The foundation of any software system is its core architecture. And too often, when companies or teams are designing the architecture of their software system, they're more interested in either sticking with a tried and tested approach that they are familiar with or attempting to adopt a cool or exciting technology in the hope of making their software appear progressive. Without fully understanding the purpose of the system and perhaps adopting an architecture that best fits it.

Software is all about solving problems and the architecture should be designed around those solutions and be made fit for the purpose of what it is trying to achieve. Choosing the wrong architecture limits the effectiveness of your solution and will likely result in long-term issues in its quality.

2) Software is not designed with testing or quality in mind

This is easily the most important thing when it comes to creating quality software. Too many companies only think about how a system will be tested, maintained, or even define their release standards only once the code has already been written. This is far too late, and companies and architects should be thinking about these things long before the first line of code has been written.

Trying to address quality when the system is poorly designed will only lead to long-term frustrations and while e some level of quality can still be achieved, the effort to achieve it is likely higher than it needs to be.

3) Testing and automation are brought in too late

It perhaps goes without saying that testing shouldn't be an afterthought. The quality experts in the team should be engaged as soon as possible and we should not start thinking about how we are going to test a piece of work when it arrives with them, but when we are in fact going to design the solution around what their needs are.

It's allowing your quality experts enough time to analyze the requirements and identify what needs to be tested and how. And then building the solution that matches that need.

4) We don't focus enough on testing as a career

Unfortunately, as with many things' software development related, testing has traditionally not been focused on as a career. And while over time this has changed, it still appears surprisingly limited in terms of growth. After all, how many CTOs and CEOs of companies have a background in testing or even understand it? Most tech leads or architects tend to be better developers, yet their knowledge of testing may be limited.

The reason for this is we often promote a strong growth and development pipeline on both the development and analysis sides of the business, but not enough focus is placed on a strong development path for testing. As a result, testers feel the need to go elsewhere for career growth. If we ensure that testers are as valued in business as any other function within the business, we can ensure they are engaged and willing to stay with companies long-term.

5) The software is not testable

Too often companies might design great software that can functionally work but is a nightmare to test. This shouldn't be a thing anymore, but it is amazing how often it still happens. Testability shouldn't just be a consideration anymore but should form the foundation of a software's design. This means code needs to be designed in functions that can be easily automated, that functionality should be built into APIs and stored procedures rather than frontend objects, and where UIs are created, that tags should be specific to the needs of the tester's specifications.

It also means that how data and input flow in and out of code is consistent and specified clearly within the requirements and adhered to. Consistent and standardized design is just as important as reliability and teams need to conform to these standards and not do their own thing.

6) A lack of learning

The aim of any quality team is defect prevention instead of defect detection and correction. Inevitably teams are going to make mistakes along the way, and we are going to build things that don't quite meet the lofty standards you set for yourselves and your customers. In cases like this, it's important for teams to take the time out to learn from their mistakes.

I have found in many teams and organizations, often one of the key things lacking is a sufficient attitude towards looking back, understanding why issues occurred, and mitigating them for the future. Instead, many teams just jump to the next sprint or task ahead with the hope that everything will go smoothly next time and end up repeating many of the same errors all over again. A quality-driven team on the other hand is prepared to slow down, take the time to reflect, and focus on getting better and improving as a team before they rush off to their next task.

7) Teams are not incentivized on quality

If you think of what teams and companies will often pride themselves in, it's in their ability to deliver quickly, the number of lines of code they write, or the innovative solutions of their tech. These are things that drive a lot of people in the tech industry.

Having software with as few defects as possible sounds a lot less cool and unfortunately, the same sentiment often applies to the way teams are measured or even incentivized through personal goals. If you want your team to build quality software, you need to make it a priority and measure this accordingly.

Whether a person is a product owner, developer, analyst, or tester, they should be measured on the quality of their software. I do understand that part of the issue may be that teams do not know how to measure this. I will cover some ideas of how quality can be measured in a team in a later chapter on Developing Models for Quality Maturity.

There is a saying in the performance-driven world that you are what you are measured against, and this certainly applies in the tech space where quality can only effectively be delivered in software when we make it a focus for teams to aspire towards.

8) Process quality gates do not place enough emphasis on quality

At any stage in the software development process, individuals and teams have a definition of what constitutes a definition of done. Although we often don't think too much about this, a definition of done is just as important as the details of a user story or task itself as it will dictate the measurement by which we determine a person is truly completed with their work and should move onto the next task.

This is where we need to be specific in what is needed from a quality perspective and where we should be placing emphasis on ensuring that every task is performed with the right quality outcome.

I again into detail on quality gates and the definition of done deliverables later in the book.

9) Your leads do not understand quality and testing

It's difficult to build quality into a system or even test any system appropriately if we don't fully understand what this entails. Sadly, for all the University degrees out there, not many focus on either of these issues and as companies, we don't place enough emphasis on building up the understanding of these areas either. And when the leads in a company, whether technical or not, don't understand what it takes to build and test quality software, it's likely they will place much emphasis on it lower down.

If a Product Owner, Tech Lead, or even higher-level manager or CTO aren't collectively focusing on building quality into a solution upfront, it's going to be incredibly difficult for a company to get this right later. If you want to build quality software, get experts who can help to train and provide this insight and, if possible, ensure that a quality expert is high enough in the company structure to drive this from the front.

10) You are not budgeting enough money toward quality development and testing

As you will see a lot as you continue going through this book, designing high-quality software is not easy nor cheap. In fact, to do something right takes more effort than to do something quickly and as a result, you need to be prepared to absorb these costs.

And I'm not just referring to monetary here, though this is definitely included, but in sometimes slowing down on your delivery to build things correctly or placing more emphasis on building automated testing systems which are often just as tricky, if not even more complicated than the code they test.

Don't take it lightly- if you want quality you need to invest in it.

11) Lack of accountability

Now, I am not saying here that teams, or people, should be chastised when they make a mistake. Rather I would encourage teams to be solution-focused than trying to point out errors and find fault with others. What I mean by lack of accountability is that there needs to be clear traceability and guidelines within a team on who is responsible for what. When protocols fail and it's not clear who is responsible for what, things will fall through the cracks.

This also has the unintended impact of limiting teams' abilities to work cohesively together. As teams will end up looking to place blame elsewhere and not take ownership for certain errors rather than taking ownership and looking to improve from their mistakes.

12) You just don't see the problem

Ultimately many companies just don't take software testing and quality seriously enough. They might think they do, but a lack of deliberate focus on it will eventually prove otherwise. Companies that don't place emphasis on designing software correctly, allowing teams to design it correctly, and investing heavily in the right testing frameworks will inevitably lose out in achieving their goals of designing quality software.

Make a change

Driving quality in any organization and pinpointing the challenges is not as simple as I've made it sound. Though I'm pretty sure that you could define many quality issues within any organization into one or several of these categories. Over the rest of this book, I will look into certain aspects of software design, testing, and quality culture to assist in better understanding how you can move from these failures toward a successful quality culture.

Or perhaps you are still a young company or team still in the early phases of development. If that's the case, then you can get the head start you need to build these principles into your products and teams from the beginning and ensure not just quality in your initial offering, but long-term as well.

As long as we're prepared to learn from the past to look for better paths in our future. Then we are already making the first step to improvement.

The Story of the Belter – A Story of Deliberate Design

Early in my career, I was taught a very valuable lesson that has served me well to this day. That of the Story of the Belter. A simple story, but one that certainly changed the way I think not just about software development, but many of the things I do personally as well.

The story is not meant to be technical at all and can apply to pretty much any profession. However, in this chapter, I will help you to understand how it has impacted me as a software developer and tester and can help you design better software. Shaping a lot of your design thinking to be clearer and more quality focused.

But first, let me tell you the story of the belter.

The story begins with a young, ambitious employee. Eager to rise in the business world and make a name for himself. And while he starts his career with much enthusiasm, over time he becomes frustrated by his lack of growth and feels upset that those around him appear to be progressing faster in their careers than he does. Disgruntled, he decides to confront his boss and complain about his situation and ask why the company is not promoting him.

Thinking about it carefully, his boss decides that rather than simply just explaining it to him outright, he will teach him the lesson firsthand. He asks the young employee to do him a favor and once complete he will give him the answer. He asks them to go down to the ground floor of the building where a new store was opening and find out what the store is. The employee thinks little of the request and so goes down to the ground floor, looks at the signage, and returns.

"It's a leather belt store." The employee declares triumphantly as they return. Feeling satisfied that this task has been satisfactorily accomplished, no matter how simple or small it may have been.

"Great thanks. I am looking for a new belt. What type of belt styles do they offer?" The manager replies.

The employee, rather perplexed, realizes he doesn't know the answer and so goes down to find out. Upon returning he informs his boss that the store sells frame, box frame, plate, and ring style belts. For both normal suit pants along with suspenders.

"Excellent", his manager replies. "And what colors do they come in?"

The employee once again realizes he doesn't know the answer to this question so goes back down to find out and returns to provide his manager with a list of belt colors on offer.

However, his manager is not yet done and proceeds to send the employee down to find out both the price of the different belts, how they accept payment, and whether they deliver.

After the sixth trip down to the shop and back, the young employee is remarkably frustrated and angrily reminds his manager that he has done what was asked and is therefore owed an answer.

The manager agrees, but to provide an answer he decides to call in one of the colleagues who was recently promoted and provide them with the same task. Asking them to go down to the bottom floor and find out what the store was. The employee proceeds to ask a host of questions about what sort of information the manager requires, which the manager duly provides.

This allows the newly promoted employee to make a single trip down to the store and return with the exact information the manager was looking for the first time. Impressed the manager thanks the employee and sends him back to his desk.

Turning to the frustrated employee now, the manager provides him with the answer, telling him that while he did complete his task, it took him several attempts to get it done while the other person got it right the first time.

The difference between the promoted colleague and him lay not in their ability to do the work, but in how the one approaches their task to find out all the information and get it right the first time, rather than just answering the immediate questions which were asked of them.

It may be a simple story, but it has an important lesson for all of us. The story of the Belter teaches one about the importance of gathering information and fully understanding the problem before one tries to complete a task. It reminds us about the importance of asking questions and trying to understand why a task needs to be done, before simply just trying to solve it.

So, why does it matter to software quality? Because rather than focusing on just building the software, we need to spend time fully understanding the details of what is required, why we are building it, and indeed what it would take to build it correctly. It's about assessing the requirements and needs of the software, both from a business and technical perspective, and getting these right before we start building the software.

The importance of requirements analysis is nothing new and has been around for many years in the software development and testing world. But in a move toward companies becoming more "Agile" and focusing on faster delivery, proper requirements analysis and testing have fallen by the wayside. Binned because it was mistakenly labeled as a waterfall process. Instead, we've now replaced detailed requirements with more generic user stories without realizing the importance that the requirements provided long term in building the software right.

And this is nothing against the idea of user stories. Writing stories and requirements from a user perspective is indeed something we should do. There is also nothing wrong with taking time out in our sprints to experiment and find out the best way to build things before committing to a final approach.

The problem is that while the Agile software development approach was designed for quicker and more immediate feedback between clients and businesses to reduce scope creep, we have stopped the requirements process altogether. We have shifted the problem away from scope creep being incurred too late in a project cycle because a solution didn't operate like intended, to scope creep now occurring because the details were too vague in the first place.

And while I'm not going to ask us to go back to a time when a 100-page document was written and carefully review multiple times before any project work even started. I do think we need to do a better job at asking a lot more questions about the software we are building and documenting many of these specifics in a way that makes it clear exactly what type of system we are building.

The following are questions you need clear answers to before you should consider a story ready to work on:

Know why you are building it

Every project you work on serves a purpose and every function that is worked on should exist within the application for a reason. Understanding this is vital to ensure that you are not building it with the correct intention in mind but will also define how it should be used and tested and therefore form the guide of your quality criteria.

Essentially what you are trying to do here is understand the mind of your user and how they will intend to use the feature you are working on. Thinking about this may also allow you to form a guideline for how the software should behave, perform and also scale based on usage scenarios.

It's information that affects your architectural approach to building your applications, how they will run in production, how you will approach coding them, the structure of data needs and tolerance to certain things like security and performance. And this is without even thinking of how the software will be tested, supported, and maintained before it makes its way into production.

Know what you are building
Having the why in place is ultimately incredibly important, but all this should lead you to build a better system, and more specifically, you need to understand as a team how you intend to build this. This means understanding how its individual parts are supposed to work, what information should be handled via APIs and what will the UI do. Knowing how your data should be shaped, stored, and preferably utilized should also form part of this.

It's okay to not know all the detail around this. As teams should be allowed to work on the details along the way or figure them out as they work on them. However, there should be at least some high-level conceptualization of this, otherwise, it's likely that your development effort will be wasted and your quality, especially, compromised due to a lack of clarity on how everything should be built and tested.

Do you have enough information to test it?
Essentially, after getting the answers to these two previous questions. you want to be left with enough information in which to know how the software should be tested. This means having enough information to know what type of tests are required, what the data will look like for those tests, what permutations are required to test, and how is the

application supposed to work under certain error conditions. Yes, that might sound like a lot of extremely specific information. But then, that is the point.

If you have all this information, then you probably have all the information you need to be successful in writing your code. The best part of this approach though is it will help you to discern the things you don't know and therefore work on them better. This is essentially the whole philosophy behind Test-Driven Development and there is a good reason why it is popular. If we write tests upfront with clear assertions to what attributes will pass or fail a piece of code, we write better code.

We tend to not place enough emphasis on the coverage these tests might achieve and may not give enough thought to every possible permutation. Something which we need to do, as much as possible.

Do you understand all the dependencies?
Understanding how your team and your piece of functionality under test works is important. But seldom is any piece of code completely isolated. So, it's important to know how other systems, APIS, databases, etc. are intending to use your code and, similarly, what other functionality you are reliant on for your code to work. This ensures that you have a clear idea of not just how to test your piece of code, but also how its integration and end-to-end tests will work.

Documentation shouldn't be a bad word

Once you can answer these above questions, you probably have enough detail for the team to begin their work. Writing tests and developing to the requirements with little confusion between them.

However, it's not just about having good analysis in place. It's also making sure that everyone else understands this good analysis and to do so effectively, you need to ensure that several key criteria are documented (either in some tool or even in the code repo).
I know documentation can be a bad word to many a developer, but the truth is that having clear direction makes developing software a lot faster and resolving conflicts in our development process, a lot easier too.

Again though, there is more to it though than loosely jotting down certain decisions and rules somewhere. To ensure that requirements will be able to trace directly to the code, the tests and be in a way that can be maintained and changed along with the code, the detail requirements need to meet the following criteria:

- **Clear and Unambiguous** – The requirements are easy to understand by all and don't leave room for misinterpretation.
- **Complete** – Have all the information needed to meet the testability requirements
- **Consistent and Non-redundant** – The information is documented consistently and the same way across the system, so that other teams and people can easily understand them and find them many years later if needed.
- **Modifiable and Traceable** – If requirements need to change, it should be easy for teams to be able to alter the specific requirements with the impact of

this change and the tests/code affected by it, easy to identify.

- **Prioritized and Measurable** – Not all parts of a system are equal, and a team should know what the most crucial parts are to get right and which aren't so that they can make the necessary risk-based decisions should they need them. Similarly, what it will take to meet or achieve specific requirements is important.
- **Include both the business and technical details** – Don't just have your business analysts write the business purpose of the requirements, but the technical reasons for the approach and design of the software and what criteria it needs to meet.

This latter part on technical requirements is key. As we learned in the chapter on Defining Quality, there are a lot of non-functional requirements to consider. And detailing these is arguably the most important aspect of any formal design process. And why I feel we need to shift more engineering effort towards the planning process to ensure we get our software systems better structured to allow them to meet the quality goals we want to achieve.

This means both a closer collaboration between analysts and architects in documenting what needs to get built, but also arguably for analysts themselves to become more technically minded and have a greater awareness of the architectural principles that need to be followed to achieve a greater quality design.

We simply cannot escape the effort put into understanding our different problem spaces better and how the software we are building needs to meet this need. And ensure we then provide our development teams with as much information as needed to start work on their project. It sounds time-consuming, and it's not always fun, but if you get it right, the resulting software will serve the business purpose far better. And probably make for a happier development team who enjoys working with the system.

Let's learn from the story of the Belter

Don't be like the employee who needed to go back and forth many times before they were able to complete the task successfully. Rather, let's prioritize asking questions, learning, and working to deliver software right the first time.

The Importance of Traceability

As development teams look to be more responsive and agile in their processes, one of the key initiatives is to reduce waste. Identifying what waste to reduce is not always easy and sometimes we identify the wrong things to be removed. One of those common areas where we look to cut waste is in the use of decent requirements repository, test management, or defect management tools. Sadly, these are the very things that they should actually be looking to hold onto as they are perhaps the biggest clues to efficiency that teams need. And the main reason why is traceability.

What is traceability and why is it so important?

Traceability is history and as any historian would teach you, the study of history is not just about the past, but an opportunity to see what you can learn from the past that will improve your future. Similarly, if we do not keep records of our past and where our errors are, we are likely to remake them in the future and not move forward as a development team. And repeating mistakes is the most inefficient way of developing software. Yet, we too easily fall into this trap anyway.

So what traceability are we looking for?

Well, it may vary from team to team, but if you cannot recall over the past few release cycles which user stories have caused the most issues, which tests failed the most, what their root cause is, and which functionality or type of functionality was affected the most – then you are likely to repeat all those same mistakes. And as cumbersome as management tools might appear, they are the best sources of providing this information.

So, while we need to improve our efficiencies and minimize waste across the board when it comes to clunky processes – we should not use this as an excuse for not following test best practices. If we are not keeping full traceability of our requirements, test, defects, and areas they impact, we are probably going to make those same mistakes repeatedly. And while you might think you are saving a lot of effort and time; the quality of your product and the satisfaction of your customers will suffer.

Never underestimate the value of a good process. There are many things we can do to improve the way we work with tools and reduce the efficiencies of the processes we have, but don't cut this one out entirely.

Below are some examples of the different types of traceability that you get and how they add value to your software project:

1. Forward Traceability
Forward traceability refers to the verification of requirements. This is where your requirements are linked to specific tests and measures (at code coverage, performance, or security scanning level) and tells the business that all tests relating to these requirements have been met and that this specific requirement is ready for release.

This is both helpful to the business as it makes it easy to track the development of a project but also vital to the team because it allows specific tests to be written to ensure all aspects of the requirements have been met and then have the developers design their code to go about meeting those requirements.

Forward traceability can also be used to see the impact that specific requirements or coding changes have on the testing impact, as teams can see the impact of these changes lower down and this helps them to better understand the risk of these changes and leads to smarter decision-making.

Forward traceability forms the basis for any test-driven development as well, as all the tests should be identified and scripted based on these requirements, though tests can also include a wider range of non-functional requirements that they need to adhere to as well.

2. Backward Traceability
Backward traceability refers to the linking of specific test failures and issues back to parts of the code and requirements, to help isolate where the issues may lie and speed up the fixing process.

This makes it easy for teams to gain specific context for a defect, which helps in identifying what needs to be fixed, provides them with more information for a root cause investigation, and better understand the impact that a defect has on the project. Vital information which can save teams critical time and again allow for smarter decisions to be made.

3. Prioritization

When we combine our different requirements and tests with priority levels it allows teams to make prioritized decisions on what tasks or work should be done first. Having clarity in what requirements, tests, or defects are more critical helps highlight what pieces of work should be prioritized by a team

Now that we have the benefits of this simple example in mind, we can talk about defining test traceability.

Test Traceability

When looking at traceability, it's clear that while we have the forward and backward traceability that center from requirements to defects and back, those tests remain the key criteria for what should drive your traceability efforts.

We have already established that we can link specific tests to requirements and use that as both a guide for designing tests and tracing the coverage of our testing efforts against those requirements.

This test traceability provides the confidence to verify that the application works as expected. And confidence is not something that should be taken for granted. When a team is ready to say that code is ready to go live, you want to say that with a fair amount of confidence in the testing and quality effort leading up to that point. So, being able to confidently say that testing has met the criteria for go-live, allows teams to make these decisions easily.

And it is not just about the initial development, because as the application itself evolves, the tests themselves evolve to continually verify application functionality.

Why Test Traceability Matters?
Simply put, test traceability ensures that all functionality is verified. It enables you to quickly test specific areas of the application whenever you apply software fixes, or add new functionality.

When your application is small, you know exactly what's going on when things are broken. In addition, if your development team consists of one or two people, things are simple. When bugs appear, you simply fix them. However, the more complex your application becomes, and the more people become involved with the code, the more precise you must become to identify areas that need fixing.

Traceability helps manage project complexity
Traceability might not often seem like a big thing when we are thinking at a small level, but as teams and our software grows and becomes more complex, you will find it will add a lot of value to the development lifecycle of your system.

Keeping track of many different individual services, multiple application versions, and working with the interdependencies within large systems become tricky and if you have the correct traceability in your testing it again helps the team to understand the impact of changes across all the different elements of these bigger systems ad can help to make sense of this complexity.

Traceability makes Parallel Development easier

The Importance of Traceability

I have mentioned working with multiple versions of software above, but it is not just about looking back to previous versions. In today's development world a lot of development happens in parallel and there can often be differing versions in development at any given time. And you need traceability to help manage the complexity

So, for example, while you might be working on a new feature that will form part of a version A of your product, there may be additional work on other projects that will also touch your particular services and form part of later B, C, and D versions – all with differing go-live dates, but all with developing overlapping at any given point.

In this scenario of parallel development, the team must know which login tests to run against which version of the application. When testing version A of the application, they should run the tests appropriate to version A. When testing version B or C of the application, the team must then ensure they're running login tests appropriate for these versions.

This helps to ensure that you are testing smart as a team and helps to isolate any issues or defects that make only arise in certain versions of the code.

Traceability with Automated Testing Brings Confidence
Current CI/CD practices integrate and deploy new code very often. As a result, the system changes frequently. That means maintaining system stability while ensuring that the application meets business requirements becomes a delicate balancing act. Having automated testing in place ensures system stability and integrity as the system changes with development efforts.

Traceability allows us to have the confidence to know that our CI processes and respective tests are meeting the needs of the business, even through all the volatility of daily change and delivery.

While traceability should form part of all tests done on or software systems, it's important that we look at automated tests across different levels. And considering we normally work on our unit tests first; we need to ensure that we first build traceability not those lower-level tests before looking at higher-level tests.

Something which is often the opposite of what you see many teams doing as the testers focus on traceability only in their end-to-end and acceptance testers with developers not focusing on this at all, or very little. But if we want to make use of the full benefits of traceability in helping us build better software, we need to start traceability at a unit test level first before looking at higher-level tests.

Unit Tests
Before code is even written, teams should start scripting their unit tests and integrating them into the build process. Even when actual business requirements don't go into detail on how specific modules should work, developers should understand what the code is supposed to do and how it plays its part in verifying these bigger requirements.

All these tests should then be linked directly through your tooling to those end requirements. We can either do this directly or break up our main requirements into smaller technical requirements for more granular tracking and better prioritization. However, doing this helps us to think through our development process better ad ensure that every part of the code we are writing serves its intended purpose with the desired outcomes clearly defined.

Once efficient unit tests cover most application code, confidence in system stability rises. Using modern tools, developers can understand how much of their code is covered with testing. This way they can trace unit tests.

Multiple-Layer Tests

The next layer of automatic testing creates automated tests that span several layers of the application. As compared to unit tests, multiple-layer tests span the API layer to the domain objects and storage layers. They test a slice of the application and thus cover the integration of the various layers of the application.

Teams can trace groups of requirements to these multiple layer tests as they span a lot of the codebase. At the same time, unit tests that form the foundation of these layered tests should also be linked, so that we can ensure our tests at the required layer when the lower layer tests are successful, but also to help identify issues when failures do occur.

User Interface Driven Tests

UI Driven tests may be the most complicated to automate, given the fragility of UI systems over procedural and reliable backend systems, slower performance, and the fragility of unmocked environments. However, from a traceability perspective, UI tests are often the easiest to link back to the original requirements, given that most analysis focuses on the user experience and therefore makes it easy to trace acceptance to a UI-driven test.

However, a common mistake is an overreliance on UI tests for acceptance criteria. While UI tests are easier for any analyst or product owner to go and validate themselves. You want to keep that separate from the actual criteria the technical development team uses and keep much of the focus of your tests at a lower, technical level. Leveraging those as the basis for higher-level acceptance tests at a UI level.

CI Execution
I've spoken about linking your requirements, code, issues, and test altogether. However, our tests need to be executed several times a day – or at every build – and the best way to track all of this is in your CI tooling. Each fresh build or pipeline execution should be tracked with traceability showing which parts of the code and tests were executed in each (and thereby which requirements or issues may have been touched during this time).

Many CI jobs may not actually involve any change and the likelihood it brings different execution results to its underlying code is minimal. But it can help to pinpoint changes in other dependencies or environmental issues that occur at various times. History is again a vital aid here and correlating project issues to builds is a great way to better understand the deployment minutiae of your software system.

I do understand though that tracking execution for every CI job can be extremely taxing from a data storage perspective and so it's important to clear out this data on a regular basis and rather use it to form trends that oy u can learn from unless you're working through specific issues in which case you may want to store as much execution information as possible.

Database Layer

Another very common functional area that gets easily forgotten by many development teams is the database layer. With the focus on functional validation lying with the developed code, the data layer can easily be overlooked. And even if checking the DB forms part of the testing, you want to ensure that there is clear traceability between the code and the database areas that it covers.

This makes it easier for teams to measure test coverage at a DB level, better debug data-specific issues and perhaps test deeper at a data layer to cover a wider range of use cases. It can seem like an unnecessary bit of overhead to include specific SQL or DB information in your testing details, but it can add a lot of value in delivering a quality data layer in your system and reducing future maintenance efforts.

Invest in traceability tooling

Having all these layers of testing that cover your application code will require some tools that can help you maximize your confidence and keep track of your testing and requirements. And the more complex and the higher the number of systems in operation and development and the more you want to ensure there is clear traceability in place.

While some traceability tooling can be unnecessarily expensive, especially in how they want to integrate all the requirements and testing into their software and lock you in place, there are a lot of open-source solutions that can help with this, with many CI tooling also catering for this to varying degrees. What matters more is not so much the tool itself, but rather ensuring that you cater for it within your testing frameworks itself and that a way to link across your different requirements, tests, CI pipeline execution, and issues exists.

Traceability is not just about linking information to testing and then storing the data for historical purposes. But also provides you and your team with critical information about the effectiveness of your development process and quality delivered across all the aforementioned layers. Using a variety of filters and dashboarding, if you have effective traceability tooling in place you can pinpoint specific issues and understand impacts clearly without needing to do an intensive investigation and the time it can save in helping to identify ways teams can improve is invaluable.

Test Tracing Proves Things Work

I know that having 100% test coverage for an application is a lofty ideal that often comes into conflict with the daily pressures of delivering software. However, having a clear testing strategy with an efficient way to trace application functionality to actual test cases will bring strong confidence in your product. In the end, test tracing proves applications work ... or don't when things fail along the way.

Traceability Matters

The Importance of Traceability

Making use of traceability in our projects, across all our layers of testing and linking them to our requirements and defects plays a vital role in understanding our systems better ad how we can design them better. So, even though traceability is often the last thing on many organizations' minds, it's vital to invest in tooling or frameworks that can help achieve this and build into the processes that allow you as a team to get the best out of your tracing.

Selecting an architecture that fits

Having clear requirements and an understanding of a system is vital, as it will help to ensure the software is correctly designed for its purpose. And this is where we need to consider the architecture that needs to be adopted for the problem space.

If the system you are designing is part of a pre-existing application ecosystem, it then means you need to decide how best to structure your architecture to best meet the needs of its purpose within the existing organizational ecosystem. If the system you need to design is something that is standalone, then you have the freedom of designing something that could adopt the right architecture for its purpose.

This is an important step, as often companies can tend to default to their existing architectural approach or choose to adopt a popular trend in the software development world, like microservices or blockchain – without fully understanding the benefits of a specific architecture and whether it is fit for purpose.

As system designers (whatever your role, even though this might be something traditionally left to Architects, a team approach should always be preferred), it's natural to focus on the big picture of how a system, or combination of software systems are structured and fit together. However, I'll be the first to admit that there are so many ways of designing software that it's easy to be very narrow-minded on the one or two approaches you are familiar with, without fully broadening your approach and identifying other structures which could actually be more suited to the problem you are trying to solve.

So, with this in mind and as a result of a lot of research I have conducted myself on the different approaches and methodologies I have come across over the past few months, I would like to share my thoughts on the different popular software architectures out there and when one might be better suited to your needs.

What makes an architecture?

Before I get too far into the different types of architecture though, I think it's worth defining exactly what software architecture is.

Well, most commonly it refers to the structure of your different software programs. A guideline to whether your system is broken down into small chunks or operates as a bigger piece in unison. It determines the rule and protocols by which the whole system should communicate and how data, security, and endpoints are defined. It can also be extended further to include the choice of programming languages that a system should be developed in and the different rules applying to that, as well the overall structure of the code, linting, testing, and even its deployment and repository configurations. So, in essence, almost everything.

However, for the purpose of this chapter, I am going to be focusing only on the basic structure of a software layout and how the different pieces of software should fit together. In determining the other complex decisions around tooling and programming languages, I will suggest that you study the different programming languages and their compilers in determining what would work best for you. This is a complex topic and with such a varied number of programming languages, there is no way we would be able to focus on this sufficiently.

Though, while programming language is vital and understanding how to structure your code to best optimize for it is important, the biggest determinant in how well your software will perform will come from its core architectural structure, which I focus on here.

In short, software architecture can be defined as determining how the pieces of a complex puzzle fit together. While every part of a system is different, they need to fit together to form one bigger system (or complete puzzle) and software architecture is the design process of ensuring the pieces fit together to form a complete whole and not an incomplete puzzle.

The Different Types of Architectures:

There are many ways of defining architectural patterns, but to keep things simple, I am going to focus on the bigger core patterns. With each section, I will describe how it works and when you should consider it, while also looking at some of the core benefits and caveats of each architectural pattern.

No matter how much certain people might out new and upcoming architectural patterns as a game-changer and give you many reasons why your company should coni adopting them. The reality is that every pattern has its purpose. And rather than follow trends, we should utilize the right architecture for our system. Regardless of its popularity.

In each of the below architecture types, you can further break them down into smaller micropatterns and align them with principles of other patterns. This is all perfectly acceptable.

The main idea of this chapter is to give you a high-level understanding of what the core patterns are about and why and when they should be considered. Understanding these principles will then allow you to make the adjustments in micro-patterns based on those principles and the benefits derived from them. That should help you shape the best architecture for your solution.

This is not an extensive list of different architecture types, as that would be too exhaustive. But I do generally find that most architectural methods are based on one of these concepts. So, if you can understand these architecture types well and how to apply them, then you can likely apply their design principles and different pros and cons to other architectural structures too.

I also don't spend any time talking about specific quality or test approaches for each architecture type and the reason for that would be clear when I get to the chapters that focus more specifically on testing frameworks. And that is because our testing frameworks need to be architecture agnostic and cater to all different types of software architectures. So, as you go through these different software architectures, worth keeping in the back of your mind whether your existing test approaches can cater to a particular design or not.

Layered architecture

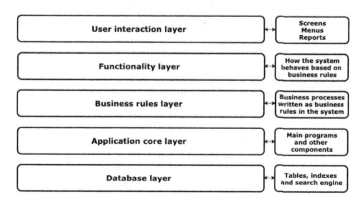

This approach is probably the most common because it is usually built around the database. And many applications in business naturally lend themselves to storing information in tables. This is something of a self-fulfilling prophecy though as many of the biggest and best software frameworks—like Java EE, Drupal, and Express—were built with this structure in mind, so it is inherently the architecture that comes most naturally to mind, and which people use most often. Whether they know it or not.

In a layered architecture, the code is arranged so the data enters the top layer and works its way down each layer until it reaches the bottom, which is usually a database. Along the way, each layer has a specific task, like checking the data for consistency or reformatting the values to keep them consistent. It's common for different programmers to work independently on different layers.

As an example, most of the popular web frameworks follow a layered architecture. Just above the database is the model layer, which often contains business logic and information about the types of data in the database. At the top is the view layer, which is often CSS, JavaScript, and HTML with dynamic embedded code. In the middle, you have the controller, which has various rules and methods for transforming the data moving between the view and the model.

The advantage of a layered architecture is the separation of concerns, which means that each layer can focus solely on its role. This makes it:

- Maintainable
- Testable (especially from a User-Driven perspective)
- Easy to assign separate roles
- Easy to update and enhance layers separately

Properly layered architectures will have isolated layers that aren't affected by certain changes in other layers, allowing for easier refactoring. This architecture can also contain additional open layers, like a service layer, that can be used to access shared services only in the business layer but also get bypassed for speed.

Caveats:

- Source code can become big and messy if it is unorganized and the modules don't have clear roles or relationships.
- Much of the code can be devoted to passing data through layers without using any logic. This can also make it slow from a performance perspective.
- Layer isolation, which is an important goal for the architecture, can also make it hard to understand the architecture without understanding every module.
- Coders can skip past layers to create tight coupling and produce a mess of complex interdependencies.
- Monolithic deployment is often unavoidable, which means small changes can require a complete redeployment of the application or a the very least, in-depth testing of the entire system.

Best for:
- New applications that need to be built quickly
- Enterprise or business applications that need to mirror traditional IT departments and processes
- Teams with inexperienced developers who don't understand other architectures yet
- Applications requiring strict maintainability and testability standards

Event-driven architecture

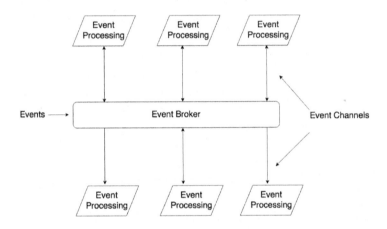

Many programs spend most of their time waiting for something to happen. This is especially true for computers that work directly with humans, but it's also common in areas like networks. Sometimes there's data that needs processing, and other times there isn't.

The event-driven architecture helps manage this by building a central unit that accepts all data and then delegates it to the separate modules that handle that particular type. This handler generates an "event," and delegates it to the code assigned to that type.

As an example, programming a web page with JavaScript involves writing the small modules that react to events like mouse clicks or keystrokes. The browser itself orchestrates all the input and makes sure that only the right code sees the right events. Many different types of events are common in the browser, but the modules interact only with the events that concern them. This is very different from the layered architecture where all data will typically pass through all layers.

Overall, event-driven architectures:
- Are easily adaptable to complex, often chaotic environments
- Scale easily
- Are easily extendable when new event types appear
- Caveats:
- Testing can be complex if the modules can affect each other. While individual modules can be tested independently, the interactions between them can only be tested in a fully functioning system.
- Error handling can be difficult to structure, especially when several modules must handle the same events.
- When modules fail, the central unit must have a backup plan.
- Messaging overhead can slow down processing speed, especially when the central unit must buffer messages that arrive in bursts.
- Developing a system-wide data structure for events can be complex when the events have very different needs.
- Maintaining a transaction-based mechanism for consistency is difficult because the modules are so decoupled and independent.

Best for:
- Asynchronous systems with asynchronous data flow

67

- Applications where the individual data blocks interact with only a few of the many modules
- User interfaces

Microkernel architecture

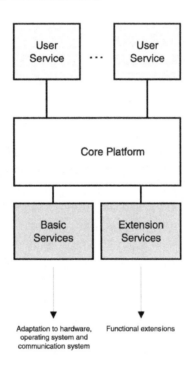

Many applications have a core set of operations that are used again and again in different patterns that depend upon the data and the task at hand. The popular development tool Eclipse, for instance, will open files, annotate them, edit them, and start up background processors. The tool is famous for doing all these jobs with Java code and then when a button is pushed, compiling the code and running it.

In this case, the basic routines for displaying a file and editing it are part of the microkernel. The Java compiler is just an extra part that's bolted on to support the basic features in the microkernel. Other programmers have extended Eclipse to develop code for other languages with other compilers. Many don't even use the Java compiler, but they all use the same basic routines for editing and annotating files.

The extra features that are layered on top are often called plug-ins. Many call this extensible approach a plug-in architecture instead.

The solution is to push some basic tasks—like asking for a name or checking on payment—into the microkernel. The different business units can then write plug-ins for the different types of claims by knitting together the rules with calls to the basic functions in the kernel.

Caveats:
- Deciding what belongs in the microkernel is often an art. It ought to hold the code that's used frequently.
- The plug-ins must include a fair amount of handshaking code, so the microkernel is aware that the plug-in is installed and ready to work.
- Modifying the microkernel can be very difficult or even impossible once a number of plug-ins depend upon it. The only solution is to modify the plug-ins too.
- Choosing the right granularity for the kernel functions is difficult to do in advance but almost impossible to change later in the game.

Best for:
- Tools used by a wide variety of people
- Applications with a clear division between basic routines and higher-order rules
- Applications with a fixed set of core routines and a dynamic set of rules that must be updated frequently

Microservices architecture

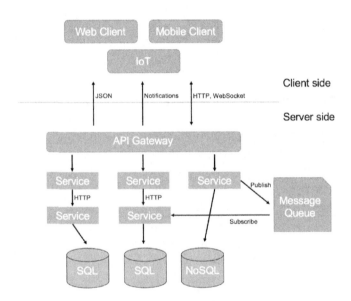

Designing software can be fun and easy in small packages, but the bigger it gets, the more unwieldy and difficult to manage it becomes. The microservice architecture is designed to prevent systems from becoming unwieldy, monolithic, and inflexible. Instead of building one big program, the goal is to create a number of different tiny programs and then create a new little program every time someone wants to add a new feature.

This approach is similar to the event-driven and microkernel approaches, but it's used mainly when the different tasks are easily separated. In many cases, different tasks can require different amounts of processing and may vary in use. Think streaming sites that need to quickly scale up and be available to a new streaming customer at any given time, independent of other users. This type of scale is what is best suited to this type of architecture.

Caveats:
- The services must be largely independent or else interaction can cause the cloud to become imbalanced.
- Not all applications have tasks that can't be easily split into independent units.
- Performance can suffer when tasks are spread out between different microservices. The communication costs can be significant.
- Too many microservices can confuse users as parts of the web page appear much later than others.

Best for:
- Websites with small components
- Corporate data centers with well-defined boundaries
- Rapidly developing new businesses and web applications
- Development teams that are spread out, often across the globe

Space-based / Cloud Architecture

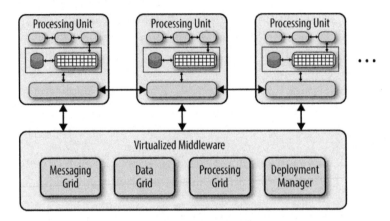

Many websites/applications are built around a database, and they function well as long as the database is able to keep up with the load. But when usage peaks and the database can't keep up with the constant challenge of writing a log of the transactions, the entire website fails.

The space-based architecture is designed to avoid functional collapse under high load by splitting up both the processing and the storage between multiple servers. The data is spread out across the nodes just like the responsibility for servicing calls. This is a similar approach that is applied to cloud computing, which is why this architecture can also be referred to as the preferred Cloud Architecture. Many companies though are unable to break down their data sufficiently to make this work effectively.

Storing the information in memory makes many jobs much faster and spreading out the storage with the processing can simplify many basic tasks. But the distributed architecture can make some types of analysis more complex. Computations that must be spread out across the entire data set—like finding an average or doing a statistical analysis—must be split up into subtasks, spread out across all the nodes, and then aggregated when it's done.

Caveats:
- Transactional support is more difficult with RAM databases.
- Generating enough load to test the system can be challenging, but the individual nodes can be tested independently.
- Developing the expertise to cache the data for speed without corrupting multiple copies is difficult.

Best for:
- High-volume data like clickstreams and user logs
- Low-value data that can be lost occasionally without big consequences — in other words, not financial or security transactions
- Social networks

Building Your Puzzle
The above information is not a complete list of ways you can structure or design your software components but does cover some of the bigger and more popular ideologies out there. In any system, it is also possible that more than one approach exists depending on need and so most often you will find a hybrid of designs speaking together. Especially in bigger and more complex companies.

Hopefully at least understanding some of the important ways you can structure your software programs will help you to better understand how your software as a company/team could better fit together and better meet the solutions you require.

Having the right architecture is an important part of building a system that is fit for purpose. With this in mind though it's time to start exploring some of the deeper design practices to show how we can build our software with quality in mind, from the beginning.

Quality Design Practices

Along with selecting the appropriate architecture for your software system, it is vital to adhere to the right design patterns as well. As we established earlier, quality is a lot more than simply having code with few defects. But also needs to meet the needs of maintainability and so we need to ensure our different systems are designed around the right principles to be robust enough to meet the various quality requirements we have already set out.

This can be achieved if we set the right goals and standards for our individual software components to achieve and then use certain design principles to achieve those goals.

The Goals of Quality Software Design

Even though there are many different ways to structure your software applications. To help ensure you are designing your software correctly, it needs to adhere to the following goals:

Correctness
Good software design means building a system characterized by a correct, conflict-free integration of all essential software elements and functionalities. Put simply, we need to build software that does what it says it does, without adding unnecessary complexities and ensure it works with all the eternal models that are required.

Optimal Resource Consumption
Software needs to operate in an efficient manner that utilizes the computing resources efficiently. Software that works

well, but taxes processors or utilizes memory too aggressively, is likely to cause a high number of performance issues over time.

Modularity and Scalability

Good software design should be easily scalable and easy to understand long after it has been delivered. It needs to be built according to the famous modularity principle widely used in all fields of engineering, with all modules arranged in layers.

Completeness

Good software design encompasses the necessary software components of modules, data objects, external interfaces, and more. All dependencies between modules and other virtual entities should be harmonized and comply with inheritance principles.

Maintainability

Software needs to not just work once off but needs to be worked on throughout its entire life cycle. Code needs to be maintainable in order for it to be improved, adapted, and maintained easily during this life span. We will look at how to write maintainable code as a separate chapter in this book.

Testability

This latter goal is one of the most important aspects of code that is likely to not be followed by a development team. In fact, you will probably not find it in many online blogs or textbooks despite its importance in software design.

Code needs to be written in such a way that it is easy to test and automate, as this will greatly speed up the testing and regression effort and allow the team to prepare code for continuous integration and deliver quality code more quickly. We will look at how to write testable code in the next chapter.

You may have noticed a lot of similarities between these principles and the non-functional requirements mentioned earlier and that's because there is a commonality in what they are achieving. Quality design practices are naturally going to give you code that will meet the strictest technical requirements and o even if your team doesn't have these technical requirements in place, ensuring that your software is designed with the right goals in mind, will provide this coverage anyway.

Design Principles for Reaching these goals

These goals for software design are great, but simply wanting code to become more modular and scalable, doesn't mean you can actually do it. This is where the following principles come in.

When correctly applied, you can apply the following principles of software design to guarantee that your software product will achieve these goals:

Abstraction
All modern software techniques predominantly involve working with abstractions of various types. Using abstractions means hiding the coding complexities and redundant details behind high-level abstractions and not delving into them until absolutely required.

This allows you to decrease irrelevant data, speed up the development process, and improve the general quality of your programming outcomes.

Most of us will have been exposed to abstraction through the principles of Object-Oriented programming, where we place code in functions, classes, or objects where they can be reused and called independently. Abstraction can be applied at all levels of the code, across APIs, UI, and even at a data layer.

Refinement
Similar to abstraction. This means getting rid of structural impurities by moving from higher levels of software design (abstractions) to lower levels in a step-by-step manner. At higher levels, the software is merely its design models. At lower levels. there will be some code. At the lowest level, the software has been completely developed.

According to this idea, refinement is an incremental process in which a team of software engineers drills down to acquire more technical details at each increment. In this way, software design is consistently elaborated without wasting time on irrelevant or side matters. In the spirit of Agile, it allows the software design and functionality to be shaped, with the more technical details shaped later.

This might sound counter-intuitive to the emphasis placed on design earlier in the book but is a particularly good approach to identifying the technical needs of your software design and goes hand-in-hand with the design process, as higher levels of refinement are done early with details only coded as they are established.

Modularity
Dividing a complex project or system into smaller components helps to better understand and manage the product. It's difficult to try and build the complexity of an entire system altogether, but if you break it up into small components which each have their own prescribed functionality, then it is significantly easier to ensure each component works well in isolation. And if these modular components can operate independently, even better.

This also makes the testing effort a lot easier, which I get into a little more later.

Everything within your software system should be pre-planned and approved with the help of engineering assessment methods. Serious systems flaws must be avoided at the beginning.

Interactions between different system components (e.g., modules and abstractions) should be the focus of architectural efforts—all of which should be seamlessly arranged within a solid software structure. Their interrelationship should be described in detail.

Patterns
Delivering pattern-based solutions is one of the most important techniques that allow software developers to achieve system predictability while saving a great deal of time. This also makes it possible to quickly deal with typical issues and apply pattern-based solutions to fix them faster.

There are three types of patterns:

- An architectural pattern occurs across software subsystems. We looked at some of these in the previous chapter.
- A design pattern occurs within a subsystem but is independent of the language.
- An idiom is a low-level pattern that is programming language-specific.

The biggest drawback of using patterns is that a lot of thinking tends to get confined to the structure of the pattern which can slow things down when adapting to a new pattern. However, once you get familiar with the pattern, you should become comfortable in applying your problem-solving logic to the structure of the pattern. The same applies when adjusting to different programming languages too.

There are a lot of different patterns and approaches out there which I won't go into detail about here. I will encourage you to do some more research on them though and decide which approaches work best for you. The structure and consistency that it gives your software solution of holistically applied though, makes things a lot easier for all the developers in the team.

Data Protection
Data must be protected from unauthorized access. Therefore, secure software development life-cycle principles should be applied and propagated throughout the entire software structure.

For example, information accessible via one software module should not be accessible via another module unless it is explicitly allowed and regulated by the software architecture plan. I do discuss how to design and code software in a secure manner later in the book.

Refactoring

Refactoring is the continuous process of bringing improvements to an internal software structure without affecting its behavior or functions. You do this through refining code in only the need layer, or even creating further layers of abstraction with the updated codebase to facilitate the improvement.

Refactoring can be a time-consuming process and does require a lot of careful thought in knowing which pieces of code to update, fix or simplify. It's an especially tricky thing to do when laid up against the expectation to deliver new functionality that adds value where refactoring can be hard to justify.

Creating a regular cycle of refactoring each sprint though allows developers in a team to keep code up to date, update and improve on a regular basis and prevents tech debt from getting out of hand.

Principles to Code Structure

The above principles are useful in the way you should approach your code design and continued maintenance. However, you still need some principles to help with structuring the actual code. This is where the SOLID (**S**ingle responsibility principle, **O**pen-closed principle, **L**iskov substitution principle, **I**nterface segregation principle, **D**ependency inversion principle.) principles come in handy.

SOLID design principles were first identified by Robert C. Martin back in 2000[1] and have become the mainstay guide to writing good code. Our technology and approach to software design may have changed since then, but the principles still stand as a fantastic way to write code.

On their own, the SOLID principles may still leave some quality gaps, but when combined with some of the directives I speak about in this book around testability, maintainability, security, and performance, it lays the perfect foundation for how to write quality code:

Single responsibility principle (SRP): A class has only one job, and only one reason to change. A class with more than one responsibility can weaken the design and lead to damage when changes occur. The SRP principle prevents the coupling of responsibilities and improves the design's overall cohesion.

Open/closed principle: This software principle conveys that after a class of code has been created and tested, it should be closed to modification, but open to extension. During the development process, requirements can change, and new functionality may be requested.

Modifying code can introduce errors into the existing code. The open/closed principle helps keep the class code fundamentally intact while allowing for it to be extended to include new functionality.

---

[1] Design Principles and Design Pattern by Robert C. Martin. Published 2000 at www.objectmentor.com

Liskov Substitution Principle (LSP): Under this software design principle, objects of a superclass should be replaceable with objects of its subclasses, meaning they behave in the same way.

For example, if B is a subclass of A, objects of B should be able to replace objects of A without undermining the performance of the program. In other words, objects of a subclass can replace objects of the superclass without impairing the system.

Interface segregation: Each class should have its own isolated interface, and class dependencies should be based on the smallest possible interface. A large and cumbersome interface with multiple class dependencies adds methods to the interface that the clients don't need.

Dependency inversion: This software principle states that high-level modules should not be dependent on low-level modules, and both should depend on abstractions. Abstractions in turn should not depend on details, but vice versa. The underlying premise here is that abstract interfaces and abstract classes are more stable than details, which are variable, and architectures built on abstractions are more stable than those built on details.

Coding is an art form, good coding is a science

I've heard the expression a few times in my career about how coding can be an art form. And there is truth to that as there is a certain elegance in the way a person goes about writing code to solve a specific problem.

Yet, while that ability to find solutions can often be an art unto itself, good code requires a more measured approach grounded in good computer science. This doesn't necessarily mean you need a degree in computer science to be good at it, but rather just that we approach it with a sense of structure and method.

I've shared some core goals that you want to follow when designing your code, along with some principles for both approach and the code design itself. These are principles that have been proven to work in the industry for many years and as such should serve you well in your development approach.

Software development is a complex art that can easily go wrong when we try to just write code that works and does not follow the appropriate principles. Yes, trying to implement the above principles does require more time and effort from the developer, but in the long run, it creates code that operates more reliably and is much easier to work with and maintain, and is likely to lead to fewer operational errors.

Writing Maintainable Code

We've already touched on the topic of why maintainable code is important. Software code has a lifespan that long exceeds the time it was first written. The computing and software industry is constantly moving forward and evolving, meaning that even legacy code needs to regularly be updated to support new technologies and software to ensure its operation. And that is only assuming if code was written perfectly the first time around and never needs any other form of maintenance, which is seldom the case. There is still the need to regularly fix issues, optimize performance and enhance security. Along with changes to functional requirements that need to be factored in.

All this means that no matter how well the code solves the initial problem it was set out to, we need to ensure that the code is developed in a manner that others can go back and easily keep it up to date, without needing to take time figuring out what is going on or rewriting the code because they are unable to do so. Activities that are unnecessarily time-consuming and potentially very problematic if there is a bug in the code and no one can easily decipher it.

There are developers that want to keep themselves valuable by trying to write "clever code" that only they can easily maintain and thereby ensure their value to the company. The reality is though that writing unmaintainable code is not a sign of cleverness or how critical your skills are, but simply poor coding and it should be seen as a merit to you and your team when they would happily go into code you wrote to update it because they know you have done a fantastic job in making your code maintainable.

The following principles should help to ensure that the code written is easier to maintain and ensure that your code lives long beyond the time you need to be required to maintain it:

Use less code

I will start with the common thread that we have seen through this book thus far – about trying to keep your code as modular and small as possible.

It makes sense to remember that the less code you have, the less there is to maintain. So, in the coding world, the phrase, "less is more" ends up being true because getting rid of untouched functions and diagnostic statements will not just make your code look cleaner but keep the context of what it does far clearer and minimize the space where code can go wrong.

And while some developers may want to try and write all their code themselves, if you have the chance to use existing libraries, even better! Although it is better to rewrite some libraries due to their low quality, some are helpful, and the established ones will often have a well-developed solution that would take you considerable effort to even just attempt to replicate. Many existing libraries though are already well-established and have their own testing infrastructure already in place. Therefore, there is less work for you and your team to maintain it.

Using existing libraries keeps things modular, more testable, and once again reduces the problems being solved in the code itself. All things which tick the box for maintainability.

Don't forget about error checking
The biggest problem with trying to maintain code can often be trying to figure out what is wrong in the first place when issues arise. Good error checking keeps your program from exploding and makes it faster to debug. When you look at a procedure where all the error checking is in order, you don't have to spend time seeking the mistake.

Fix the problem, not the symptoms
The difference between quick fixes and real fixes is that the first scenario occurs when a developer decides to solve the symptoms and not the problem. Real fixes occur when the developer understands the cause of a bug and manages to pinpoint it. Everything done hastily will only create confusing code for the next person to clean up.

While we will talk about process in more detail later in the book, it's important to mention at this point that rather than rush into trying to fix a problem as fast as possible, teams should have a proper Root Cause Analysis (RCA) process in place. Where teams take the time out to ensure they understand the real cause of issues and correctly document them. This will ensure that teams do not just implement the correct fix, but also allow teams to prevent them from happening in the first place.

Don't repeat yourself (often abbreviated to DRY).
It is easier to maintain code if it only exists in one place, and this also ensures consistency. If code is duplicated, there is a

good chance that you'll forget to update one of the copies, meaning the bugs you fix in one copy will still be there in the other copy.

There can often be a challenge here because sometimes using the same module everywhere can affect performance because the module needs to cater to a wider number of use cases rather than being optimized for each specific use case. This really depends on what is most important to your software system and as long as the performance impact is minimal, I would also look to keep things modular to remove any form of repetition.

Readable Code

And now for easily the most important aspect of making code maintainable – making it readable.

When you decide to get into the software development space you anticipate that most of your day will be spent sitting at your desk and coding all day. Sadly, this is not a reality because the truth is alongside much of your time being taken up in conversations, meetings, documentation, and admin – you will probably spend a lot more time READING code than actually writing it.

Which is why if you really want to grow as a developer – you don't just need to become good at reading – but actually writing code in a way that makes the lives of your fellow coders a lot easier, so that they – like you – can end up doing less reading and more coding every time they need to review, modify or update the work you have produced. Of course, you could always be a bit of a masochist and get joy

out of writing hard-to-decipher code for your colleagues –
though chances are that joy will be short-lived when they
throw it back at you when reviewing your merge requests.

So, I want to provide some tips on writing code that make it a
lot easier for those around you to read it and understand
exactly what is going on. This is nothing ground-breaking and
you can find similar tips available on many different
platforms. That doesn't make this any less important though
as I still see many people struggle with the concept of writing
code that is easily readable. There are many things to look at,
but with the purpose of keeping this chapter as readable as
your code should be – I will refrain from going into too much
pedantic detail and just provide the basics to help you along
the way.

As you will discover, writing readable code is a lot more time-
consuming and difficult than just writing code to get the job
done – but the benefits and reduction in future maintenance
most certainly make it worthwhile.

1) Space your code out
As a coder, if often makes sense to keep everything in as few
lines as possible – but this doesn't make it easy for another
to follow what you are doing. Rather, make things easy to
read by making use of clear indentation, line breaks, space,
and keeping to the general rule of having each line of code
only declare or do one thing.

Bad
const userData=[{userId: 1, userName: 'Jan De Beer',
memberSince: '08-01-2017', fluentIn: ['English', 'IsiXhosa',
'Portuguese']},{userId: 2, userName: 'Thembi Dlamini',

memberSince: '02-11-2016', fluentIn: ['English', 'IsiZulu', 'German']},{userId: 3, userName: 'Alwyn Smith', memberSince: '29-08-2013', fluentIn: ['Afrikaans', 'English', 'German']},{userId: 4, userName: 'Hirohiro Matumoto', memberSince: '08-05-2015', fluentIn: ['Mandarin', 'English', 'German', 'Japanese']}];

Better
```
const userData = [
 {
  userId: 1,
  userName: 'Jan De Beer',
  memberSince: '08-01-2017',
  fluentIn: [
   'English',
   'IsiXhosa',
   'Portuguese'
  ]
 }, {
  userId: 2,
  userName: 'Thembi Dlamini',
  memberSince: '02-11-2016',
  fluentIn: [
   'English',
   'IsiZulu',
   'German'
  ]
 }, {
  etc...
```

2) Make your names as self-explanatory as possible
It goes without saying that variable and method names should not only fit into a necessary standard across the team,

but it should be easy to derive its purpose and intention just from reading them. You can invest a lot of time in writing comments to explain what your code does or simply just write longer, but more detailed names that can do this for you.

Making names easier to pronounce and allowing for easy distinctions between purpose and form will go a long way in helping to understand what is going on with your code.

Bad:
protected $d; // elapsed time in days

Good:
protected $elapsedTimeInDays;
protected $daysSinceCreation;
protected $daysSinceModification;
protected $fileAgeInDays;

3)   Keep your functions short and simple
The smaller the function, the better. Having a long complex function makes it difficult to maintain in the future and so you want to keep it as short as possible and ensure that it only does one thing. Having a function with multiple purposes is going to be a nightmare to debug and maintain.

It is also helpful to throw exceptions rather than return different code-dependent errors. Exceptions will provide the right amount of detail with what is going on so that the context of it is clear and it can make the debugging aspect of your code a lot easier. This takes a lot of practice and effort to get right – but unless you like dissecting code for hours on end – you'll want to get this right.

4) Smart comments

As mentioned, you don't need to comment your code if it's written in a self-explanatory fashion – though that doesn't mean comments aren't useful. Especially if the feature you are working on remains complex or if there are consequences within the code (like long execution time) then it makes sense to include these into the comments.

Additionally, another bad thing to do is comment out code that is not working. While this makes sense while you're debugging or working on a new feature – it's not something you should be including into your code merge. You may have the intention of "doing this later" – but then why include it at all?

5) Consistency

None of the above steps would be beneficial if you changed the way your code looked every time. If possible, agree on a standard for how code should look like as a team and then stick to it. This will make the task of reviewing and reading code quicker for everyone and make the workplace a happier one for everyone.

6) Let your tests understand what is going on with the code

We have already established that code should be testable and that you want to have as high a number of unit tests as possible. A topic that I will go into more detail on later in the book.

Much like production code – unit test code should be easy to read and if you have these all in place a person can at least understand what your code is trying to achieve by the tests themselves as they can see what inputs produce certain outputs and use that to have a better understanding of how certain functions work.

Unfortunately, writing maintainable, readable code does require more effort to get right the first time, but its effort that pays off quickly in maintenance cycles. A good practice in trying to ensure code is readable is by placing many of these checks into your code repository tools so that they form part of the code review process, plus you need to get the developers to ensure they can understand the code completely without any need for a walkthrough.

At the end of the day, your skills as a developer are not showcased in how quickly or effectively you can solve a problem, but rather if you can do so in a way that is easy to follow and understand. If any of these items mentioned are not something you have been deliberate in trying to follow in your coding practice, hopefully, you can make these changes and leave your team and company with code that is much easier to work with. Your fellow developers will thank you.

Aligning Design Practices with Testability

In this chapter, I will unpack the design specifics that make software more testable, maintainable, of better quality, and ultimately better equipped to deliver on its value. While we might not always realize it, software is not naturally testable but requires specific design decisions that make it easy for testing and automation to happen at all the right levels.

Testability is the term used to describe how easy it is to write automated tests for the system, class, or method to be tested. We already know that automated tests are crucial for high-quality software; it is, therefore, essential that our code is testable.

To code for testability, you need to understand how test tools interact with a software application and typically what testers will need to test the software system in its entirety. Ensuring those measures are put in place within the design of the software.

I will say up front that designing for testability is not necessarily the fastest way of building an application. A lot of the principles that you will read in this chapter will require a lot more thought and work from a development perspective to build right. However, it's important to note that while we will often only need to write code once, with some levels of maintenance required on a regular basis, tests will be run against the software constantly.

So, even if the development work takes a few weeks extra to complete. With the implementation of these different practices, the payoff is gained long term when you can now increase your test coverage and get it running in a pipeline more seamlessly than had these measures not been in place. Without many of these measures, automation would prove challenging and manual testing will drastically slow down any development effort, so you want to keep the ability to automate code effectively at the center of your code design principles.

Focus on Small Executables
Testability also refers to how easy it is to unit test the code and much like the above design principles, requires the code to be relatively modular and independent in nature. This then allows for each logical element of the code to be easily tested with a set of inputs and the different outputs asserted to ensure that each component behaves as expected.

The trick with this really is in the small part though, as essentially you want any logic tree that is written to have its own set of tests to verify that the logic operates as expected. This may not be possible with every piece of code you are writing and often several decision or logic trees may be required to be placed into an independent module, though it is important to try and keep this at a minimum. The moment there is too much logic contained in a module of code the number of permutations required to test for each possible option greatly increases, as does the room for error.

Knowing that every decision and line of code is well tested gives a high amount of confidence in knowing that it will work as expected. This doesn't mean that it will necessarily work perfectly though as there is still plenty of room for error at an integration layer. So, your code design needs to consider the needs of bigger integration tools that target these API and UI layers as well. I will talk about the make-up of these testing tools later in the book.

It's more than just writing code in small modules though and the following principles are also critical to ensuring the testability of your software:

Discoverability
One of the first things most testers will ask of their development team is to ensure that their respective tools can identify certain objects, at either a UI or backend level. This is especially true for UI testing where tools will require a form of object-id to be unique for each UI module on the screen to ensure that the test tool can interact with the object. A lot of developers for the sake of simplifying development will have screens render dynamically with buttons or different objects having no unique identifiers.

This essentially means that the testing tool cannot reliably interact with the object and will require the testers to look to identify other traits like the location of the object on the screen or any text contained within the object to automate its functionality. This tends to make the tests more brittle, and they will likely fail more often due to an object not been properly identified than would otherwise have being the case if the objects were all made uniquely identifiable.

Observability is incredibly important, but I am fully aware that effective test automation needs to be done at a lower level, which is why most of the below points are aimed at improving a code's ability to be unit tested and thereby reducing the need for higher levels of test automation that are slower and trickier to execute.

Dependency injection

Dependency injection is a design choice that means rather than the class instantiating the dependency itself, the class asks for the dependency. Have a lost you with this? Well, you're not alone as I was lost the first time, I heard it too.

Perhaps to explain it better, I will use an illustration. Let's say you need to make use of a specific tool to perform a certain task. When we are asked to do this task, we find the tool by ourselves and once we have the tool, we use it to perform the task. However, another approach is to say that, while we still need the tool when someone asks us to perform the task, instead of getting it ourselves, we get the tool from the person that wants us to do the task.

This way, we can now instantiate the task class we want to perform and simply pass it a mocked/stubbed version of our tool in the test code. This simple change in the design of the class makes the creation of automated tests easier and, therefore, increases the testability of the code.

More formally, Dependency injection can also be described as a technique where one object supplies the required dependencies of another object.

This simple change in design thinking improves the code in many ways:

- It enables us to mock/stub the dependencies in the test code, increasing the productivity of the developer during the testing phase.
- It makes all the dependencies more explicit; after all, they need to be injected (via a constructor, for example).
- It affords better separation of concerns: classes now do not need to worry about how to build their dependencies, as they are injected into them.
- The class becomes more extensible and can now work with any dependency with little effort.

Separation of concerns
I've already mentioned that modules of code should be as independent as possible. To what extent should we take this and exactly how can we design all our complex modules of code to operate as independently as possible? Well, we do this by isolating the separation of concern in what any given module is affected by.

Domain vs infrastructure
The domain is essentially where the core of the system lies, i.e., where all the business rules, logic, entities, services, etc., reside. Whereas infrastructure relates to all code that handles some form of infrastructure. For example, pieces of code that handle database queries, web service calls, or file reads and writes. In our examples, all our Data Access Objects are part of what we call infrastructure code.

When domain code and infrastructure code are mixed up together, the system becomes harder to test. For instance, a piece of code that contains SQL logic as opposed to being dependent on a Data Access Object is increasingly more difficult to work with.

The code becomes less cohesive and not just because it's two languages contained in one function, but because it covers different responsibilities – at a database layer and at a core code layer. This class now requires test cases that cover both responsibilities and makes troubleshooting issues and the maintainability of the code more complicated.

Furthermore, when you look at things from a performance perspective, optimizing code and SQL for performance are two very different skills with two vastly different ways that compilers handle the code and so to make the performance testing and code optimization issues easier, you want to ensure these two layers are separated.

And while I've used the database layer as an example here - mostly just because it is perhaps most common – it's not just about the separation of database and functional code. Things that handle anything to do with infrastructure like drivers or networking infrastructure should also remain separate from the functional code and be left to modules of their own so that they can be tested independently.

Cohesion

Cohesive classes are classes that do only one thing. Cohesive classes tend to be easier to test. This is because fewer responsibilities imply fewer test cases and fewer responsibilities often imply fewer dependencies which in turn incurs a lower testing cost, as the reduced complexity makes the tests easier to script.

On the other hand, a non-cohesive class tends to consume a large amount of testing effort. The mocking effort to cater for all the dependencies becomes time-consuming to put together, and the high number of test cases required to then cover all possible permutations will not only take longer to script but increase the maintenance effort considerably as well.

Refactoring non-cohesive classes are, therefore, important tasks when it comes to testability. A common way to do this is by splitting the non-cohesive class into several smaller-but-cohesive classes. Each small class can then be tested separately, and the class that combines them might rely either on mock objects to assert the correctness of the interactions among the dependencies or on an integration test (or both). So, while there will still be tests that require some extensive mocking, that effort is greatly reduced, and the number of tests required to ensure successful integration as opposed to catering for every possible permutation is now reduced.

Coupling
Coupling refers to the number of classes that a class depends on. A highly coupled class requires several other classes to do its work. And much like cohesiveness, this increased complexity decreases the testability of the code.

A tester trying to test a highly dependent class ends up having to test all its dependencies together. If the tester then decides to use stubs/mocks, the costs of setting them up will also be higher than they needed to be (just imagine yourself setting up 10 or 15 stubs/mocks to test a single class).

Moreover, the number of test cases that would be required to achieve a minimum amount of coverage is too high, as each dependency probably brings together a whole set of requirements and conditions.

Reducing coupling, however, is often tricky, and may be one of the biggest challenges in software design. Both for legacy systems - which may have a high level of coupling built-in – and new systems, as coupling can often make the initial development process easier.

The impact it has on testing though will quickly outweigh that development speed through the entire development process and so it's important that we consider ways to remove coupling in our code base as much as possible.

A common coupling-related refactoring is to group dependencies together into a higher and more meaningful abstraction.

To further illustrate this, imagine that class A depends on B, C, D, and E. After inspection, you notice that B interacts with C, and D interacts with E. Devising a new class that handles the communication between B and C (which we will call BC) and another one that handles the communication between D and E (which we will call DE) already reduces A's coupling. Now A depends only on BC, and DE, making it far easier to mock and test while also allowing those coupled pairs of BC and DE to also be tested far easier

In general, pushing responsibilities and dependencies to smaller classes and later connecting them via larger abstractions is a better way to think about software design

Complex conditions

As has already been showcased earlier, simplicity is easier to test than complexity. Code that features complex conditions (e.g., an if/switch statement composed of multiple Boolean operations) requires greater effort from testers as the number of decisions and boundaries that need to be tested increases. The increased complexity of the code in general also increases the chance of things going wrong.

Ideally, you want to keep the number of decisions that are required in your code to a bare minimum and so when thinking about how your program will need to make certain decisions, it's worthwhile not looking for which path is the easiest to code, but which requires the least number of decisions to operate. Coincidentally, this may also improve the performance of the code too, albeit minor.

Changing some of these conditions though can be difficult, as the code still needs to make them somewhere. Reducing the complexity of such conditions, for example by breaking it into multiple smaller conditions, will not reduce the overall complexity of the problem, but will "spread" it over different parts of the once and make each function easier to test, increasing the overall testability of the solution, even if not solving its overall complexity.

Private methods

Private methods are another coding principle that makes it easier for the developer, but harder for the tester. As private methods can only be called from inside the class where they are defined, it means they cannot be tested independently by the tester. Now, some developers may argue that a private method shouldn't need to be tested separately as it's part of the class and, therefore simply testing the class should be sufficient. But there are reasons that you may want to test these methods separately.

In principle, testers should test private methods only through their public methods. However, testers often feel the urge to test a particular private method in isolation. One common cause for this feeling is the lack of cohesion or the complexity of this private method. In other words, this method does something so different from the public method, and/or its task is so complex, that it has to be tested separately.

In terms of the design, this might mean that this private method does not belong in its current place. A common refactoring is to extract this method, maybe to a brand-new class. There, the former private method, now a public method, can be tested normally. The original class, where the private method used to be, should now depend on this new class.

Static methods
As has already been made apparent, stubbing and mocking are very important to testing and static methods adversely affect testability, as they cannot be stubbed easily. Therefore, a good rule of thumb is to avoid the creation of static methods whenever possible.

The only exceptions to this rule are possibly utility methods which are responsible for performing routine programming tasks where testing is not as crucial and so there is more benefit to keeping these methods static.

If your system has to depend on a specific static method, e.g., because it comes with the framework your software depends on, then it would be beneficial to add a layer of abstraction on top of it to increase its testability.

The same recommendation applies when your system needs code from others or external dependencies. Again, creating layers/classes that abstract away the dependency might help you in increasing testability. We emphasize that developers should not be afraid to create these extra layers. While it might seem that these layers will increase the overall complexity of the design, the increased testability pays off.

Finally, it's worth noting how there is a deep synergy between well-designed production code and testability. There are a lot of similarities in the past two chapters that call for simple and modular design. So even if you're not convinced about the importance of testability – in which case I've done a very poor job with this chapter – just sticking to proven design best practices should lead you and your team to a more testable design.

High-quality software is only achieved when software systems are designed with testability in mind, and rigorous testing techniques are applied.

Building the right test framework

As has already been mentioned in the chapter on Defining Quality, our systems don't exist on their own and an important part of how our software systems work needs to include the testing framework in which we design to help us test them. Any quality software system is only as good as the testing around it and if we don't have a good test framework in place, then overall architecture is not going to help you achieve quality, no matter how well you've stuck to the design principles followed in this book.

And I can think of no better time to discuss this topic than straight after we have looked at designing for testability. Because an important part of designing for testability is also understanding how testing systems work and then designing an appropriate test framework in unison with your code. Too often companies wait until their applications are well-architected and near completion before building an appropriate testing framework when the reality is that it should all happen at the same time.

Now, often when we think of test frameworks, we put a focus on automation frameworks. I have decided against using that terminology because I believe all testing should become automated eventually and the foundations for any good test framework need to be built with automation in mind.

So, even if a test is executed manually, - and I do believe there is a lot of value in exploratory testing and manually testing a system – if it is worth repeating, it should find its way into an automated form. And this requires the development of a framework that will make this process easy and reliable and not cause frustration for the team, as is so often the case when it comes to test automation.

Building a Scalable Test Framework

When architecting a system, we often consider how our system will be able to scale depending on the number of users interacting with it at any point in time. Indeed, it was this very design philosophy that led to the rise of Cloud computing. However, when companies are considering building their test frameworks, they are not always considering this same principle that will allow them to scale their test automation to meet the demands of their delivery.

Too often when companies design their test framework, they look at the existing needs of their organization and develop it from there. These designs will often include ways of integrating the types of applications, technologies, and tools currently in use, as well as the number of known tests to currently formulate around.

The problem with this is that tools change, applications under test change, and the size and scale of your testing are likely to grow and diversify as your products do. When designing your automation frameworks, it is important to keep this in mind, so that while you are building a solution that will help you to deliver high-quality software in a short space of time now, you also want to ensure it meets this need for the foreseeable future as well.

So, how do we do this when we don't always know what technologies and applications lie in our future or ensure that as our testing efforts grow, our delivery is not hampered? Here are a few things to consider:

Build a Tool-Agnostic Framework

One of the biggest requirements in achieving this is to ensure your framework is not reliant on tools. A big mistake that organizations and teams make when they build their framework is to choose a tool that meets their automation needs and then build their framework around that. The problem is that tools and technologies change and what might be the best tool now is not necessarily going to be the best tool for your future needs.

Along with this, there is also a need to often utilize multiple tools based on the different needs of your software, whether it be front-end, back-end, device-specific, or often even security and performance testing. Building a framework around each of the different tools that you need is not only expensive, but a nightmare to maintain as your test grows.

Below is a short list of just some of the benefits you are likely to gain through building your own tool-agnostic framework:

- Reduced maintenance overhead long-term
- Reduce the learning curve for engineers as they only need to learn one framework
- Freedom to choose the tools you want without the need to build a new framework
- Utilize multiple test tools within one framework

- Perform multiple levels and types of testing in one framework, including functional, unit, API, security, and performance testing
- Be prepared to see prolonged ROI

One of the reasons companies do this though is down to the speed of development. Building a framework around your tool is often a lot simpler because the tools come with an inherent set of functions and features that you can easily leverage in automating tests in a short space of time.

The obvious problem with this is that you as a team then tie yourself to that tool and should you need to ever add or change a tool to your framework, you are unable to easily do this. This is difficult for companies, as they understandably want to see a fast return on any investment of effort they make (the average ROI on any automation framework is between 1-2 years, so it can be a frustration for businesses), yet in building a framework companies need to be willing to invest heavily in building these things all on their own. This might add an extra 3-6 months to the development of any framework, but the long-term benefits are easily worth it if you are willing to be patient.

How to Build Your Framework

So, what exactly do you build your framework with? Well, that depends on the coding skills in your company and the types of applications you need to test. Go with a programming language you and your team are perhaps most familiar with that perhaps fits into one of the preferred languages your organization supports. Each language has certain pros and cons and I won't go into them in this book, as that is a hefty topic on its own. What matters is not so much the language it is written in but rather how it is written.

If your organization uses mostly JavaScript for the development of their various backend or frontend components though, then it makes sense to build a framework in JavaScript, as an example, as it means the entire team only needs to concentrate on supporting one language throughout. There may be some modules where a different language is used for a specific reason, but even then, your test framework will be able to work with it, and using the more widely available skillset in the organization ensures it will be maintained and developed.

Most testing tools these days can work with a variety of different languages and even if they do not natively speak your language of choice, it is relatively easy to write a module that can translate this on your behalf. Just don't let your tools dictate the language you choose.

Choosing your language is obviously the easy part. In designing an agnostic test framework, you need to be prepared to write a lot of the following functions that tools often take care of for you:

Reporting – Determining what metrics and how you want your tests to report on.

Function Libraries – Test tools often include a wide set of function libraries that dictate how it behaves around certain browsers, UI objects, and databases. While tools can still be used for this execution, your framework needs to include functions that handle this.

Test Validation – Every test framework needs to have preset criteria for the types of things a test needs to look for and verify as passed or failed Test tools include a lot of these built-in and you will need to define these yourself.

Test Input – Your framework needs to define how tests write tests that can be translated and executed. Catering for a different type of data-driven file formats is often useful

Error Handling – You will need to develop this whether you use a tool-agnostic framework or not. Many tools though have a wide set of inherent features that assist with unexpected behaviors and your framework will need to take care of this internally.

Object Repositories – While tools can still be used to help identify and execute objects in any given UI, they often interact with objects in a specific way.

From this brief list above, it might sound like the creation of a tool-agnostic framework is practically like building your own test tool and you would not be incorrect. While you would still require an actual tool to help manipulate objects and execute your tests, you should not rely on it for anything else.

Your framework at the end of the day is a software product all on its own that should be able to be invoked by anyone in the organization requiring to do some testing. It should be built, maintained, and managed just the way you would any other product.

Modular Framework Design

So, we've spoken about the importance of not building your test framework around your testing tools, but that still doesn't give us enough information to know how it should be built.

Well, the good thing if you are a developer, is that many of the good design and coding practices that apply to the development world apply to developing a good testing framework. Especially with the focus on a modular design approach. For many testers, however, it gets a little complicated because it makes the actual design and readability of the tests a little more difficult.

Understanding the benefits of modularity is not difficult though. It's knowing what level of modularity is required and the truthful answer is - as much as possible. Yes, it might take you longer to get started with your test design because you need to build every little object, test element, and action it on a separate object on its own, but once it's done, it makes it much easier to reproduce and reuse your objects as required across multiple tests. Much the same way you would expect to build your applications that need to be tested following the same principles.

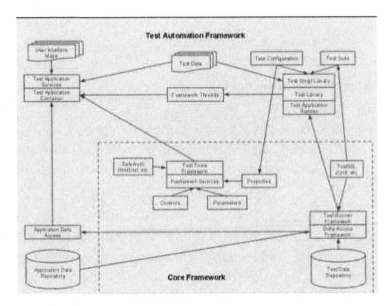

*A basic example of a high-level test framework architecture.

Treat your framework as you would any other product

However, that does lead me to one of the key things to realize when building your test framework – you are engineering a product. We expect software testers to have a different mindset from developers, but when it comes to building your actual framework, you need to treat it like you would any other product – ensure it has a clear, specified design, well-architected, and engineered around software development best practices. You should even unit test your own framework where possible to ensure any future code changes don't break other tests.

Companies are failing to build scalable and successful test automation largely because they are getting a bunch of software testers who specialize in automation to build it rather than getting a bunch of actual software engineers to code it. A good test framework will require a good grasp of development methodologies and best practices to work effectively, and it is important companies make a concerted effort to build it in such a way.

Companies are moving away from big monolithic software programs to object-oriented micro-services because it is simply easier to maintain, and your test framework should ideally follow the same design principles. And if you are using a more traditional monolithic infrastructure, having a modular design will certainly help, but you can afford better centralization that will probably better mimic your system architecture too – even though this correlation should not always be the case, as you will see from many of my points in this chapter.

Build with performance in mind

Another aspect that is often not always considered in the design of the automation framework is performance throughput. How fast does your framework execute the tests it is required to do? Again, a lot of this points toward ensuring the code is written in an optimal manner that increases processing efficiency and executes quickly. It might not seem as important as what you would need for your actual applications because it's unlikely your framework will

113

ever require the load or stress that any production application would, but still, the faster it executes, the better it can scale to your organizational needs.

All things need to be maintained

You wouldn't want to leave production code unmaintained and so you need to look after your test framework long term. It too will need to change and evolve over time and while your modular framework certainly reduces maintenance considerably, ensure that engineering hours are provisioned to keep all your tests executing as expected.

Don't take designing your test automation framework for granted. It requires careful planning, a proper software model with classes and methods, and the same level of focus you would give to building any other application. The most successful frameworks are those that adhere to the principles of sound software development.

Building a Performant Framework

As has already been established, performance is an important part of our product development as we need to make sure whatever software we are building performs at an optimal level and can handle the relevant load we need it for. We tend to forget though that automation frameworks need to be built with the same performance in mind. While it's unlikely that you will require a high load or stress on your automation framework, the speed at which it is able to execute is incredibly important, especially to ensure that it delivers the results you need in a reasonable amount of time.

More than ever in today's DevOps ready world, we want to write code and be able to run it through an automated test suite can get results in a few hours to know if it's good enough to push to production. The problem is that with thousands of different testing types, particularly those that are UI driven or End to end focused, getting any form of execution results back is likely to take many hours and often limits your ability to respond quickly to get fixes or updates into production.

There are many things that you can do though to ensure that your test automation framework executes effectively without compromising on your quality risk. Unit tests by nature are quick to execute and small in scope, but where companies struggle is with the bigger integration, component, or end-to-end tests which become a lot more onerous on execution.

The below suggestions focus mostly on this form of automated testing, though can be applied to unit tests just as easily.

Write fast-executing code

Now, this step I know is a controversial one, because I have already spoken about the benefit of writing readable code in the chapter on Designing Maintainable Code. Having code that is easy to read is far more important than complex code. From a testing perspective though with tests executed so often, we need to err on the side of being performant. Whereas tests should always be easy to understand and read, you want to follow efficient code design that runs fast.

This is a tricky thing to do but is incredibly important. We often write our test frameworks with the simplicity of test scripting in mind rather than the efficiency of execution. This is one of the reasons why a code-driven framework is effective because it removes a layer of abstraction in the processing. From a coding perspective, this means that you should avoid complicated loops that require unnecessary processing and ensure the number of decisions required in your test is kept to a minimum.

We also often tend to confuse the number of lines of code with performance when, in reality, just because your code is written in as few lines as possible, doesn't mean it is quicker when executed by a CPU. Choose the simplest form of decision-making rather than the simplest code to write.

Simplify your tests

While each test should remain independent (more on this later in the chapter), it doesn't mean you can't test multiple requirements in one test, provided there is no immediate dependency or duplication along the way. Some tests, especially end-to-end tests get weighed down because a certain element of an object is constantly verified every time a function is called, and yet it may need to be called by practically every test. Test something once, every other time that function is called, it should bypass the verify operations that slow it down. If something does fail, your error handling should take care of it.

Error Handling

A lot of the time wastage that takes place in automated test execution is a result of errors in your application or test. Your framework should be able to handle any unexpected response or system delay by failing or bypassing the necessary tests. Along with this, if a part of the code fails, yet many tests down the line call on it, your framework should be intelligent enough to ensure all subsequent tests calling that function are skipped. Another reason why your test framework needs to be modular.

Remove any latency

At times we run into problems with automation testing because we have unnecessary latency waiting for system response, especially if a 3rd party system is involved. This can be eliminated by using stub data where possible to simulate desired responses than wait for certain events to happen. It might sound like a bit of a cheat, but well-defined stub data is as accurate as production and if you are unable to work with stub data at any level of reliability it is a sign that the APIs are perhaps not defined as well as they should be.

The same applies to unnecessary logging which is great for debugging and tracking what your tests do but is not suited for use in your daily integration environment. While logging is not taxing on processing, it still adds to the processing and copious amounts of logging add up. Keep logs for debugging but try and remove them unless absolutely necessary when you release it.

Remove unnecessary tests

There can be a lot of duplication that goes into testing. From unit tests and end to end tests covering the same thing to legacy tests that while still relevant might be testing barely used functionality, remove what is not necessary. Using test design techniques like CTD (Combinatorial Test Design[2]) will also help you to identify the least number of tests to achieve a high level of coverage. Rather let your unit tests worry about 100% code coverage and design your bigger end-to-end tests using this method to reduce wastage.

Along with this is a process many companies forget about – test maintenance. Just because a test has been added to your automated regression suite doesn't mean it should stay there. Regularly review your tests and update, replace, or delete where necessary to remove anything that is unnecessary.

Performance Test your automation

And the last, but most important thing is to measure the performance of your automation and where its bottlenecks lie. You do not need to have performance tests written specifically for this, but that will certainly help. I discuss Performance testing in more detail later in the book and while I wouldn't go through too much effort trying to performance test my testing framework, I do think there is value in monitoring the execution performance and looking at ways where its efficiency can be improved – at least at a high level.

---

[2]http://research.ibm.com/haifa/dept/svt/papers/CTD_Introduction.pdf

Most integration tools can track how long each test takes to execute and teams can use this to identify specific bottlenecks and address them where possible. Do this on a regular basis and make a concerted effort to prevent long-running modules or tests from entering into your automation build. It might seem like overkill, but again this is all around building a scalable test framework and as your applications and the number of tests needed to ensure their quality grows, performance becomes key.

Again, I guess it's worth saying that you need to treat your automation framework just as you would any of your other products. It is essentially a product that is used to test your other products and the better you build it, the better it will meet the needs of your company.

Independent Test Design

A common thing that tends to break automated execution is the dependency on other tests or systems that cause unnecessary failures or prevent a multitude of tests from running. In order to ensure your automation pack mitigates this, you need to ensure each test can run independently – without putting a strain on your performance. The following below tips should help in ensuring your tests are suitably independent to be fully scalable.

Each test must be able to set itself up

Each test should be able to get the system to a point where it needs to execute without needing a process of previous tests to set up reliance accordingly. This is all pretty easy to do, but difficult to get right in a way that doesn't mean simply repeating setup and shut down steps during each test phase.

This can be done by preferably identifying a condition that a test can easily check to determine if the necessary setup already exists for a test to proceed. If it does, proceed with the test, if not – there should be a simple JSON file or config job that can be round to get it to where it needs to be. This can be done by using SQL to change system settings, but as SQL performance is often slow, using some form of config file or JSON file would be ideal.

The trick to making this work is ensuring the condition that identifies if a setup is required is an easy one to process. A fast way to do this is to have a simple flag setting in a file that is set or not. Try not to do this in tests themselves though as this creates dependencies that can cause problems if previous tests set the flags incorrectly. If possible, this should be something on the application under test itself that can be easily read through the API that doesn't require a DB or UI check to determine this.

Tests should be short, simple, and specific

I've mentioned this before, but tests should not be long-winded, but quick to execute, with a clear objective. This can be difficult for end-to-end tests which often try to step through a series of processes together to determine its final success/failure. A lot of the processes should be able to be configured through API or config file changes which should mean that the test can still provide a full solution perspective, but test only what it needs to do. Those other steps should be tested in their own procedures, specifically through unit or component tests, and not form part of the end-to-end tests. Don't repeat your tests, it's a waste of time.

You might argue that what is the point of doing end-to-end regression tests if you aren't covering the full functionality. I would argue that if your unit testing cannot test it to expectation, then the fault is there and should form part of an end-to-end test. End-to-end or solution tests should rather focus only on those things unit tests will never get to or that unit testing is not cannot verify accurately, but at the same time. Repeating steps that exist in the unit tests should be unnecessary and using preset configurations should achieve this.

Tests should be traceable

The reason a test should execute should be clear in the way it is mapped back to specific product requirements, and it should be evident that when tests failed, exactly which product requirements are affected by this. This is not something you would typically build into your automation framework, but rather in your code deployment tool that sends an XML file to your test management tool.

Along with traceability to requirements and defects, each test should report on its status- whether passed, failed, or blocked and take a snapshot and details of the error wherever possible. While the steps to do this should be called from separate functions, each test should report on its progress before moving on to the next test. This ensures that you have peace of mind and understand the behavior of your tests better. Having a set of tests not report their progress does not give you confidence in your failures. It might not seem like this last step should relate to test independence, but again it's all about your tests being able to give you the full picture regardless of when and how they execute.

Traceability also helps you to identify when tests are no longer required and can be removed from your regular regression run.

A good test of knowing whether your tests are suitably independent or not should be to execute them both on their own and as part of a larger pack and they should execute equally throughout. In your debug logs though you should be able to measure when test setup occurred or not and the execution time of your test to know if the measures you are putting in place are effective.

The beauty of having tests that run independently and efficiently is that you can scale your execution as you need and even have multiple tests executing against different instances of your system without needing to worry about interdependencies. We expect our applications to scale with use, why not our tests too?

So, as you have probably already established. There is a lot of work that needs to go into a test framework. Using tools out of the box with their built-in functions is unlikely going to meet all your organization's needs, provide some added maintenance, and also create a dependency between you and the service provider.

This is not to say that there are many organizations out there that don't offer great tools and approaches to test and automation frameworks. Just that it is better for you to build the right framework for your company and ensure it provides the modularity, performance, and independence that you will need for your testing to provide a lasting value to your development efforts. And help you to drastically reduce the effort placed on keeping your test framework maintained.

Anatomy of a Testing Framework

So, I have spoken about what a good testing framework requires, but like with other forms of software architecture, there needs to be an understanding of how test frameworks typically work to build a framework that will best suit your company's purpose.

So, in this chapter we will focus on the cope anatomy of an automation system, understanding the important elements of what forms a working testing system – before narrowing other focus to the framework and tooling itself to have a better understanding of what these should look like too.

Understanding the Testing System

First, I will begin by unpacking all the different elements that make up a Test Automation System. In simple terms, a test system can be defined as a set of processes, standards, and interactions between the components in which scripts are designed and executed. I want to focus on this first over and above a typical framework because most people automatically jump to thinking of an automation framework when they hear the world framework, without realizing that all the systems involved in testing are far bigger than that and effective framework design should cater for all these elements.

Also, rather than give an opinion on how I feel these should be applied, I will rather just define the different elements and allow you to then formulate a solution that best suits your organization. The purpose is to allow you to identify what is important in building a strong automation framework that suits your products and then setting standards in place to allow you as an organization to make use of them correctly.

1)   System Under Test

The first component of any automation system lies not with the automation itself, but the system that you want automated. After all, before you should even begin to look at how to automate your system, you need to consider the different components of your system and understand how automation can impact them in the first place.

The reality is that the success of many a company's automation efforts starts with the system itself. The automation strategy that needs to be applied is largely dependent on the design of your system. If you have the privilege of designing your system from scratch, then there are best standards by designing smaller modular API-heavy systems which are more conducive to good automation. However, this is not always the case, and your automation framework should ideally be built around the automation needs of the system under test. Trying to approach it from the framework first is going to simply lead to frustration.

2) Automation Scripting Framework

This is the time when many companies might choose to start shopping around for tools, but what is needed first is an actual design of how your automation is intended to look, including standards that should be adhered to when building the necessary scripting framework.

Many times, when automation fails in organizations, it is not necessarily due to a lack of skills or poor tool section, but often because of a lack of adherence to set standards and coding best practices. There is no shortcut to quality automation and so you need to ensure that proper standards are put in place to make this a reality. This is why when talking about the actual scripts themselves, I emphasize standards so much.

There are many things to consider when designing your scripting framework, but the below things should all be considered:

- Handle scripts and data separately

Automated test scripts should be clearly separated from the input data store (e.g., XML, JSON files, Flat files, or Databases), so that no modifications are required to the test scripts whenever data must be changed for multiple input values.

- Coding Standards

Scripting standards should always be maintained across the test automation framework, which will discourage individual coding practices and help in maintaining code uniformity, which makes it easier for software testers and developers to interpret.

- Extensibility and Maintenance

An ideal test automation framework should steadily support all-new enhancements to the software application and allow modification of existing features e.g. A reusable library can be created, which would help in enhancing application features with minimal effort.

- Script/Framework Versioning

Versions of framework/scripts should be maintained either in a local repository or versioning tool, which would help in easy monitoring of changes to the software code.

- Library

A library should contain all reusable components and external connections such as databases, generic functions, application functions, etc. Software testers should be exposed only to the implemented libraries and tests should be performed by invoking these libraries.

- Levels

Your automation framework should not just focus on a level of automation that testers are traditionally involved in, but apply to the entire software, meaning that unit, contract, component, and integration tests, across both frontend and backend, should all fall under your strategy with an approach tied in accordingly.

3)   Testing Tools

It's only once you understand how you plan to build your framework that you should then only consider the appropriate automation tool. As previously mentioned, too often companies tend to approach automation by looking at the tool first and then building around that when in reality, a tool is simply just a means to enable interaction with an object or application.

While choosing the right tool is important (especially when licensing fees are involved), it should not be your primary driver and it's better to fit a tool into your framework and strategy rather than the other way around, otherwise, you may find yourself locked into a tool that is perhaps not fit for purpose and increasingly irreplaceable.

I also want to add at this point that there is another reason why I choose to focus on my scripting before a tool. Because true test automation needs to be scripted and driven from the code and not some in-built feature-set. Relying on a tool to provide you with a working framework not only locks you into the tool for the foreseeable future but also limits you to the capabilities of the toolset, rather than allowing you to build precisely what is needed.

There may be many vendors that offer a low code/no-code automation solution, but these tend to not work unless you only intended for your automation to be bare bones. If you want deep coverage and high-quality automation that is highly reusable, then you will need to apply a programmatic approach to your automation efforts.

4) Project, Defect, and management tools

It's not just about the execution of your testing, as there are a lot of other critical aspects to software testing that need to be managed. From the requirements and scope to the delivery and, importantly, the defects. These are all tools that need to be considered in how your framework fits together to ensure there is traceability between all of them.

I have already spoken above about how important traceability is to software quality and so for your testing framework to best support this, it needs to ensure that it is able to easily integrate between these different tools, without being overly reliant on them. Making use of the various tool APIs is helpful for this, along with an understanding of the different information that is important to the quality effort. More on this latter part later in the book.

5) Processes

Lastly comes your processes. Like every component in the automation framework, this is also important and if you are not going to get this right, automation will continue to frustrate you. First up, proper automation takes time, and it needs to be provided within the development cycle to be built correctly. Much of this focus should be on building automation work across all areas of the stack in work planning with automation seen as a set definition of done before you can expect automation efforts to be taken seriously.

Testing is also a culture that requires the whole team to contribute to this. The more unit tests developers right the fewer integration tests are likely required by the testers making their automation loads easier. It also requires getting clarity on functionality early and the team is willing to work around the extra overhead of automation if needed.

Testing is complex, which is why it remains such a problematic focus for many organizations. However, if you want to make a success out of your testing approach it's important that you get all the different components of it working together.

Digging deeper into the automation framework

So, now that we have a better understanding of what the overall system entails, let us have a look at a typical test automation framework and what components it typically needs to cater for to be useful and adaptable to your organization.

At its very simplest definition, a test automation framework is an integrated system that sets the rules of automation for your application under test. It will essentially serve as an integration point for function libraries, test data sources, object details, and various reusable modules. While some record and playback tools may combine these systems, you will want to keep them separate to make them reusable and allow only for the relevant components to be updated rather than an entire suite.

1) Interface Environment

At the core of your framework is essentially what is called an interface engine. This forms the foundation of all your scripting and is code that dictates how test cases are translated into actual executable code and interact with the system/s under test. This will obviously dictate the programming language that forms the foundation of your framework, though the environment and engine (below) can also be designed in such a way as to work with different programming languages to cater to a wide variety of tools, applications, and skillsets.

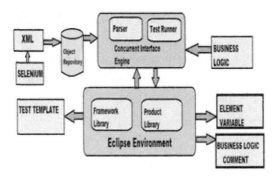

Above: Example of an automation framework using Eclipse and Selenium

The environment should also include the following important aspects of your automation system.

- Function libraries

It should contain a set of shared functions that are available to all people that they can use for a variety of things related directly to their interaction with both the system under test and the tests themselves.

- Test data sources

One of the most important aspects of testing is data. We cannot get outputs from our software without the different permutations of data providing input and how we manage this data should form a large part of our framework. For small unit tests, a lot of this can be easily mocked but the bigger and more complex the scenarios, the more likely you will need to rely on large quantities of data that need to be customer representative, but also not be actual customer data for security reasons. Your framework should contain both rules and methods for dealing with this, preferably with an actual integration to test databases where data is regularly created/updated with the right amount of data for the scenarios required.

- Expectation Management

More than simply just being code that serves up data and checks the output, a test framework should be clear in how expectations or, more specifically, assertions are handled. The guidelines around where and how to assert different types of objects and mapping these back to the business requirements are important and your environment should provide the technical management of this.

- Reporting

The interface environment needs to make it clear exactly how test results are stored and displayed. This will often depend on the engine and how it works, but ideally, you want some form of consistent visualization here to report back on the effectiveness of the test executions and provide a trend on runs and common issues where possible.

2)   Interface Engine

Interface engines are built on top of the Interface Environment and perform the actual execution of the tests. This is often performed by the relevant testing tools that have been chosen but can also be scripted independently. All frameworks will require some form of engine though to perform the actual. The interface engine consists of a parser and a test runner. The parser is present to parse the object files coming from the object repository into the test-specific scripting language. The test runner executes the test scripts using a test harness. I will uncover how these work in a little more detail later in the chapter.

3)   Object Repository

Any test framework will need to be interaction with objects of the system under tests, whether it be actual API endpoints or UI elements on a screen. These details should all be storied independently of actual tests so that should the underlying objects get changed or updated, the tests shouldn't need to change themselves.

So, these might be the big three aspects that make up your standard automation scripting framework, but they are far from the only things to think about. Your framework also needs to consider the different types of scripting techniques you are planning on following as well, ideally focusing on the one that will allow for the fastest and best maintainability scripting in your organization.

Various framework/scripting techniques are generally used:

- Linear (procedural code, possibly generated by tools like those that use record and playback). Very easy to follow and keeps the test well contained, though leads to a lot of duplication of test steps across many different tests.
- Structured (uses control structures - typically 'if-else', 'switch', 'for', 'while' conditions/ statements). Another fairly readable test approach, though having decision trees within your test code can lead to more errors in test execution and complicate your test framework unnecessarily.
- Data-driven (data is persisted outside of tests in a database, spreadsheet, or other mechanisms). This framework requires the test harness to simply send data to a specific object or endpoint and then validate the response. It creates a nice separation between code and test data, though keeping the test data up-to-date can be tricky, especially when data is reused across different tests.
- Keyword-driven. This is a very popular approach where keywords are used to translate certain more readable lines of a test into an automated function. This makes tests more readable to non-coders and

gets them included in automation work, though can create a maintenance nightmare

- Hybrid (two or more of the patterns above are used). Given that there is no one perfect approach to test automation that suits all scenarios, it's common for a chosen test framework to utilize different approaches.

There is no set rule for which framework works best and most often you would want your test automation scripting framework to be a hybrid, as you will need some aspects of your framework to be structured or linear (unit and component tests) and others to be data-driven or keyword-driven (integration and end-to-end tests). This also depends on the skill level of the testers in your team, with the data and keyword driven approaches also offering ways for testers to create tests without needing extensive coding knowledge.

So, I will leave the decision-making up to you, but hopefully understanding the different aspects of your test automation system and scripting framework will help you to make the right decisions and perhaps also prepare you for the final part of this chapter, which is the anatomy of a test automation tool.

Anatomy of a Test Automation Tool

It may not seem like a primary focus for many companies where the focus is on rightly implementing the correct framework. However, with tools often coming at a cost, its important people be empowered with understanding how they work a little better to ensure they make the correct decisions about them. This is especially important when there are currently so many different open-source alternatives to the more established products which may often work better for companies if they are able to harness their capabilities effectively.

In this part of the chapter, I want to unpack the basic anatomy of automation tools and some of the things that differentiate them from each other. As there are many different tools out there the intent is not to evaluate tools against each other or necessarily cover aspects of every tool, but simply just give you a high-level perspective of how automation tools are designed to work. And by work, I'm not referring to how you use the tools and automate them, but the actual architecture in works that make them able to do what they do.

While automation tools differ vastly between Web-Based UI, Desktop UI, API, or unit testing tools, they all generally consist of the same principles. At its very core, a test automation tool is an application or piece of code that serves as an interface between your test script and the application under test. While for unit tests, this is easy to do because it is essentially a piece of code that executes the underlying code to check its output, tools that test a full application work a little different.

The components generally consist of a parser, which acts as the code interpreter or compiler, an assertion library that provides a variety of functions that allow for the verification of outputs, and runners which enable the actual execution of your test cases.

135

1) Parsers

Essentially, a parser is a compiler or interpreter component that breaks data into smaller elements for easy translation into another language. A parser takes input in the form of a sequence of program instructions and usually builds a data structure in the form of a parse tree or an abstract syntax tree.

The overall process of parsing involves three stages:

Lexical Analysis: A lexical analyzer is used to produce instructions from a stream of input string characters, which are broken into small components to form meaningful expressions.

Syntactic Analysis: Checks whether the generated instructions form a meaningful expression. This makes use of a context-free grammar that defines algorithmic procedures for components. These work to form an expression and define the order in which tokens must be placed.

Semantic Parsing: The final parsing stage in which the meaning and implications of the validated expression are determined, and necessary actions are taken.

A parser's main purpose is to determine if input data may be derived from the start symbol of the grammar. If yes, then in what ways can this input data be derived? This is achieved as follows:

Top-Down Parsing: Involves searching a parse tree to find the leftmost derivations of an input stream by using a top-down expansion. Examples include LL parsers and recursive-descent parsers.

Bottom-Up Parsing: Involves rewriting the input back to the start symbol. This type of parsing is also known as shift-reduce parsing.

2) Assertion Library

An assertion library is essentially a function built into the respective automation tool that allows for a variety of checks or conditions against the expected outputs. For API testing, this can be very simple in terms of just checking that certain fields can exist and then expands more with UI testing where it can recognize and verify against the various state of objects.

The whole purpose of assertion libraries is to remove the need to code a variety of functions to check against certain outputs and essentially makes it easier for testers to verify aspects of an object under test without needing to do extensive coding, which is often the reason many companies go with the different tools, to enhance the development of their test scripts.

Assertion libraries vary between tools in how they work and are often mostly customizable at a unit test level, but how they work applies consistently across them all.

3) Test Runners

A test runner is the library or tool that picks up an assembly (or a source code directory) from the parser, that contains unit tests, and a bunch of settings, and then executes them and writes the test results to the console or log files.

Often tools may make use of different runners' dependent on the code or tool in operation. In Selenium, this would typically be your web.driver for a browser, but there are many runners that tackle things for different APIs and programming languages for unit testing (NUnit, JUnit, MS Test, etc.).

These differ in their architecture, but should each contain something resembling the below:

- Describable

A describable is essentially a function that gets specific information about the object it is interacting with to know what to execute and what not to.

- Run

A run function is essentially something that executes code. It compiles the test script as code and then executes it in the provided framework. It is designed to execute a given piece of compiled code against a target code and return a relevant result.

- Parent Runner

A Parent Runner is an abstract base class which essentially allows the handling of multiple runs. Any testing suite is likely made of multiple tests that need to be executed against the different aspects of code or executable objects and a parent runner is what handles the execution of these individual run jobs, intercepts their logs, and stores them in a log file.

- Reporter

While the parent runner may handle the execution of multiple individual runners, these essentially each pass-through output which needs to be collected in various log forms. A reporter function takes these logs and collates the information in a way that can then be read. While some tools may provide a form of default graphical reporting, most test frameworks will be scripted to handle reporting in their own way and so these reporter functionalities are not always utilized but remain an aspect of the tool that can be useful.

So, whether you are utilizing commercial software as part of your tooling or building your own, it important that you understand how to utilize those tools as part of your testing framework to build a framework that will properly meet your needs.

Know where To Test

This book may be mostly about designing software right to reduce the impact of testing. And just as I mentioned in the chapter on testing frameworks that your test code is as important as your production code, I would be remiss to not talk about how to test the software.

Testing is still a vital part of the software development process and if we don't respect the approach to testing software, we won't be able to properly build quality software. Software testing remains the best way to verify that software works correctly and find flaws in our software design. And even when software is designed correctly, software is complex enough that inevitably there will be things that we cannot build correctly without effective software testing to expose these gaps to us.

Software testing is a complex science and more than just a verification process of checking if things work once the team are done with their development parts. For one, software itself is complicated and there are so many permutations and considerations to consider in any one system, that you can't simply just verify that things work.

There are so many more technical details around the system, functionally, architecturally, performance or security-wise, and the intended business use that is needed to ensure quality in this regard. However, at the same time, no piece of software is ever truly done and with software development very much an iterative process where small enhancements are added on a daily basis. So, automation and efficiency become very important. And to ensure you maximize that efficiency without jeopardizing the quality of the system across all of its layers, it is vital that you know how to test the software in the most appropriate fashion.

To start off, I will begin with providing a high level of places that you should be testing and then will write additional chapters which will go into specific details on other areas of testing, like Unit, UI, API, Database, Security, and Performance.

The different layers of testing:

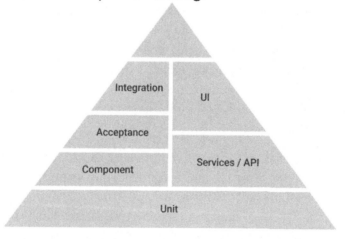

Many people should be familiar with a testing pyramid such as this one. It is reasonably self-explanatory with any solid testing foundation built on a greater number of tests in the lower levels so that less testing effort is required higher up where the complexity and cost of the testing effort are significantly higher too. Something which we have already explored previously in the book.

The truth though is that while this pyramid might be well known, it is not very well applied, with many companies still placing far too much emphasis on the higher levels of the pyramid rather than testing various aspects of a system where they should be.

So, let's investigate the different layers of the triangle and explore how testing should apply there.

Unit Testing

The most important, but often least utilized, aspect of testing strategy is the unit test layer. It's essentially code that tests the code. Simplistic in construction and design, but actually the one where the most emphasis should be placed, because it's the easiest to automate and where you will achieve most of your test coverage in the shortest space of time.

However, it's not just because they're fast to write and execute that makes them important. Because they are closer to the code, they are also easier to debug, identify the error and maintain as it aligns actual code changes to specific unit tests. Offering fantastic benefits to traceability of your coverage and test execution.

While they require a fair amount of coding knowledge to write effectively, they are the easiest tests to write, focusing simply on calling functions, inputting values, and asserting on those outputs. At times there may be a fair amount of mocking to mimic the operation and interaction of other components but once these frameworks have been implemented, they remain easy to maintain. I cover these in more detail in the next chapter of this book.

Component Testing

Like unit tests, but rather than focusing on small modules of code, they group several functions of code together as part of a microsystem or microservice and still make use of mocking to provide a decent level of coverage.

Component tests can be more difficult to script, require detailed knowledge of how the system works, and are often time-consuming to put together. Why they remain important though is because of the types of defects they catch. Whereas unit tests ensure that your code works in isolation, component tests remove much of this isolation and focus on testing connected components of code. And how differing modules of code operate together is often entirely different from how they may behave in unison, even with controlled mocks in operation.

These tests should allow the tests to target a higher coverage layer as they may expose parts of the code that were other missed in unit testing. These are also tests that – like unit tests – need to be fully automated and put into deployment pipelines.

Component Tests are the closest you will get to full integration tests without the need for an actual integrated environment and as such, make execution in an automated pipeline a lot easier.

Know where To Test

Contract Testing

Contract testing is a very lightweight test that is perhaps most relevant for APIs but can also be utilized by stored procedures, databases, and micro-frontend components. These tests are essentially just tests that look for the relevant fields with which it needs to integrate with to ensure that the fields it requires for integration are still exactly what is required. These tests are used to test for breaking changes when other teams might make a change on a system and not be aware that it may affect another system. They differ from component tests in that connect to external unmocked systems and provide that first layer of sanity testing to ensure two components or microservices will interact with each other.

Integration Testing

This is typically where most of the dedicated software testers will apply their focus, and where code is deployed into a shared environment and put through testing with other components to ensure they work correctly. The focus of this testing is using relevant data and actual system responses rather than mocked and controlled spaces and testing a few scenarios across the entirety of its journey.

The idea of testing at this layer is not to test an extensive number of scenarios but rather to ensure that a system works as close as possible to the way a user/customer would use it. They are time-consuming to script, slower in execution through a pipeline, and require detailed data to execute effectively but remain necessary and increase in importance the larger the system.

Acceptance / End-to-End testing

Very similar to integration testing but the larger the system the more it encompasses. While a small system would probably have its integration testing serve the purposes of a full end-to-end system, a large system of many multiple microservices and applications will probably have different levels of integration testing before one big end-to-end phase of testing where the entire system is put together. In big companies, this may be manual as opposed to automated due to the complexity of all the moving parts and the effort that it takes to build reliable automated tests at this layer, but if companies can build their systems right from the ground up, even the largest systems can have this entire process automated.

Verification Testing

You've tested your system, but you still need to deploy it into a production environment or as close to a "production-like environment" to ensure it works. At this point, the software has already been extensively tested, but you want to ensure that it remains operational, especially when changes occur on an infrastructure or operating system level.

These scripts are lightweight but should target critical services to ensure that nothing major is broken when these infrastructure changes are made. They don't need to complete a full user journey - especially if targeting a production environment directly - but should be able to ensure that all parts of the application are operational and can connect to each other.

Tests of this nature are also very good for support teams looking to monitor production environments where they can schedule them for regular execution and respond quickly to events when they fail and report failures. When tests at this level fail, you would typically want to trigger a form of alerting to ensure systems are brought back online as fast as possible.

DB, API, and UI Testing

We have explored the left-hand side of the pyramid, but there is also the right-hand side where things like Databases, APIs, and UIs exist, and these also need to be tested differently. Much the same way you would approach your levels of testing differently, so you need to approach testing these aspects of your system differently.

I go into these layers in more detail in the following chapters, as each of these areas has a lot to unpack and makes use of component, contract, integration, and end-to-end testing in different ways.

Where is regression testing in this list?

I haven't spoken about regression testing in this mix because it really is something that falls within all these areas. Additionally, with the move towards more automated testing, it shouldn't just become a thing of what tests form part of your regression because they all should form part of your regression. All these tests should be automated and therefore execute on a regular basis rather than a traditional regression cycle. And the more a system relies on unit, contract, and automated integration testing, the faster and more regularly a team can execute this automation with little difficulty.

Don't underestimate the importance of each layer

Now whether you are approaching testing from a front-end or backend perspective and regardless of the architecture of your system, you should ensure that all these testing phases are considered. Just focusing on one aspect is likely to leave gaps in your testing approach and therefore the quality of your software.

The Need to Test Smaller

I wanted to include this section in the chapter because I think it offers an important mind shift for many people in how they traditionally approach software testing. Especially if you are a software tester yourself.

The historical approach to testing that many testers are taught is that to ensure you have great test coverage across your test suite, you need to think of the bigger picture. Understanding how a bigger system works helps you understand its different dependencies, usage patterns of customers, and context that leads to solid and more accurate test design and therefore why testers may operate separately from developers to come up with different test approaches. The problem is this is all wrong.

Yes, understanding the greater system does indeed help understand things better, but testing the bigger system is neither efficient nor the most-quality centric approach to testing. Instead, as the testing triangle shows us, we need to rather ensure we have a strong base of unit tests upon which to build our testing rather than take a top-down approach.

Rather your testing resources should be focusing on how the individual components of code are built and prioritize testing efforts on this. The closer to the code you can test, the better it is for your overall solution. This may be a radical change for many software testers especially, but if they can learn to do this effectively, they can save themselves massive amounts of testing effort in the future and help build better quality software. I expand on this in more detail in the next chapter where I discuss not just how to approach unit testing, but also why you want to make use of critical test analysis skills at this layer of your testing efforts.

Diving Deeper into Unit Testing

As we explored in the previous chapter, Unit Testing forms the bottom of our testing pyramid and should be where the majority of our tests reside.

While I go into detail on some of the other forms of testing later in the book, I do want to spend some time on unit testing and the testing actions of the development team. Because good quality code is the foundation of quality software. And testing it properly at this level plays a bigger role than all other aspects of testing. Though this doesn't take away from other forms of testing, which are still needed and critical parts of the software development process.

Sadly, I have often found this not to be the case, with a majority of companies and teams placing greater emphasis on trying to approach their software testing from an end-to-end phase and thinking of the solution in its entirety rather than testing at the smallest levels of the code. Even those companies that do place emphasis on unit tests have their developers committed to writing unit tests and don't get the testers involved in them at all. Essentially this means that the testing experts in the team are not even involved where the majority of tests are supposed to reside.

When I first made the transition from software developer to tester, the big trend was to keep testers and developers separate to ensure the independence of the testing team. This concept of "not marking your own homework" was seen as a strong purveyor of quality, but over time many companies have realized that this created more problems than it fixed. For instance, as a tester, I would end up focusing on how to find faults in the software, rather than how to build it better. It also meant that my goal as a tester was not aligned with the developers' which naturally meant that I would work separately from them.

These days I've learned that the best way to build high-quality software is to get it right at the design level. The best way to do this is by designing your software in a manner that suits your testing strategy and allows for small, easy-to-maintain components that allow for decent unit testing. It is also important to test as close to the code as possible by playing in the unit test space because this is where the majority of testing efforts need to be focused.

Which is why, before I actually go into the specifics of how to write an effective unit test, I want to make sure that I drive the point home that you need testing specialists focused on this layer of testing and not just keep them focused on the other more complex forms of testing.

Why should testers focus on a unit test?

As a person who has spent the majority of their career in testing, one of the first mindset changes that I required for unit testing was to shift focus from the big picture integration of the software to the details of the code. By doing this, I saw how systems can be better mocked and isolated to allow the unit test to be effective.

If you are a tester and have not made the transition to intensive unit testing, this might be because you are not yet convinced of its benefits over-and-above the regular high-integration test coverage that testers look for. Perhaps knowing some of the benefits will help get you there:

Collaboration

The most important benefit is that it will force collaboration between developers and testers. So, if you're a tester, and you wish that you could get more involved in how the software is designed, then getting involved with unit testing is the best place to start.

Ever since I've been involved with the unit tests, I have developed better relationships with developers and the work they do and worked together with them on assessing the quality of the product.

It also ensures that the development team hits the required test coverage needed to reduce the integration testing that can be done elsewhere.

Facilitate Test-driven development (TDD)

TDD is a big buzzword that calls for the tests relating to a developer's code to be clearly identified and written before they've finished their development work. This makes it easy for them to know what their code is supposed to do and the parameters it needs to pass in order to be deemed ready for the next phase of testing and deployment. Unit tests help with TDD by making it easy to associate lines of code with tests and thereby identify exactly which parts of the code are not behaving correctly.

This helps developers when they want to submit their code and know that it's met all of the relevant criteria almost immediately. It also helps developers to think more clearly about what they're designing, as the guidelines and criteria to pass are clearly understood.

Finding bugs early

Not only are unit tests faster to execute, but it also means that defects are found the moment code is pushed into the pipeline. This means that the developer can see the failure straight away and get it fixed before the code even makes it into any form of integrated test environment. This will likely reduce the number of defects elsewhere and the amount of wasted effort teams are usually spending on logging and fixing defects later in the development cycle

Reducing costs and duplication

Faster execution and early error detection are going to save efforts later in the development cycle, making it cheaper for everyone. This reduces the duplication of covering the same scenarios at an integration level that developers cover in their unit tests.

Documenting the code and increasing traceability

Another benefit, which should appeal nicely to testers – but also the whole team - is that unit tests make it easy to identify what the code does while allowing for traceability – which is vital to ensuring software quality.

Most coding repositories will allow software requirements to link up to unit tests. This helps testers track coverage a lot easier without them needing to do this themselves – again saving a lot of unnecessary effort.

Improved ideation

One of the things that I have found with testing is that not everyone does a good job at it. This is why we have testing experts in the first place. Not all people have the knack for thinking of good test scenarios, so the quality of code and tests can vary greatly.

By getting involved in unit tests and focusing on isolated use cases, a tester is more easily able to apply their testing mindset to identify better test scenarios for the team and think of many scenarios they might not have thought of otherwise.

What Should be Unit Tested

So, hopefully now that I've convinced you that unit tests should not just be the domain of the developers right the code, but something which testers need to get involved with as well, let's go into specifics of how we should approach unit testing in the first place.

Testers typically like to test everything when the code arrives in their environments. However, when there is confidence that the code is correctly tested at a unit level, the tester can focus on high-priority and complex scenarios instead. Before jumping into unit tests, it is also helpful to understand what scenarios are best suited for unit testing. While you want most of your testing to be done in this way, there is still a need for integration and end-to-end tests that ensure the individual parts all behave correctly and in unison.

Entry and exit points: All code receives input and then provides an output. Essentially, what you are looking to unit test is everything that a piece of code can receive, and then you must ensure it sends out the correct output. By catching everything that flows through each piece of code in the system, you greatly reduce the number of failures that are likely to occur when they are integrated as a whole.

Isolated functionality: While most code will operate on an integrated level, there are many functions that will handle all computation internally. These can be unit tested exclusively and teams should aim to hit 100%-unit test coverage on these pieces of code. I have mostly come across isolated functions when working in microservices architecture where authentication or calculator functions have no dependencies. This means that they can be completely unit tested with no need for additional integration.

Boundary value validations: Code behaves the same when it receives valid or invalid arguments, regardless of whether it is entered from a UI, some integrated API, or directly through the code. There is no need for testers to go through exhaustive scenarios when much of this can be covered in unit tests.

Clear data permutations: When the data inputs and outputs are clear, it makes that code or component an ideal candidate for a unit test. If you're dealing with complex data permutations, then it is best to tackle these at an integration level. The reason for this is that complex data is often difficult to mock, timeous to process and will slow down your coding pipeline.

Security and performance: While the majority of load, performance, and security testing happens at an integration level, these can also be tested at a unit level. Each piece of code should be able to handle an invalid authentication, redirection, or SQL/code injection and transmit code efficiently. Unit tests can be created to validate these. After all, a system's security and performance are only as effective as its weakest part, so ensuring there are no weak parts is a good place to start.

Writing Effective Unit Tests

It is one thing knowing why you should focus on your unit testing strategy and what to unit tests, but none of that is helpful if you do not write effective unit tests. For the sake of both developers and testers, these guidelines will help you ensure that your unit tests are written effectively, and in a manner that testers can contribute to easily.

To determine whether a certain scenario would be suited for unit testing, use the following characteristics to help you:

Fast: It is not uncommon for mature projects to have thousands of unit tests. Unit tests should take very little time to run - milliseconds even.

Isolated: Unit tests are standalone, can be run in isolation, and have no dependencies on any outside factors such as a file system or database.

Repeatable: A unit test's results should be consistent; this means that it should always return the same result if nothing is changed between runs.

Self-checking: The test should be able to automatically detect if it passed or failed without any human interaction.

Timely: A unit test should not take a disproportionately long time to write compared to the code being tested. If you find that testing the code is taking a large amount of time compared to writing the code, consider a design that is more testable.

If your specific scenario does not suit any of these, it's likely that it would be best tested in another way, at a place higher up on the testing triangle.

The following guidelines should assist teams in writing effective unit tests that will also appeal to the needs of the testing team.

1. Naming your tests

Tests are useful for more than just making sure that your code works, they also provide documentation. Just by looking at the suite of unit tests, you should be able to infer the behavior of your code. Additionally, when tests fail, you can see exactly which scenarios did not meet your expectations. The name of your test should consist of three parts:

- The name of the method being tested
- The scenario under which it's being tested
- The behavior expected when the scenario is invoked

By using these naming conventions, you ensure that it is easy to identify what any test or code is supposed to do while also speeding up your ability to debug your code.

2. Arranging your tests

Readability is one of the most important aspects of writing a test. While it may be possible to combine some steps and reduce the size of your test, the primary goal is to make the test as readable as possible. A common pattern when unit testing is "Arrange, Act, Assert". As the name implies, it consists of three main actions:

- Arrange your objects, by creating and setting them up in a way that readies your code for the intended test
- Act on an object
- Assert that something is as expected

By clearly separating each of these actions within the test, you highlight:

- The dependencies required to call your code,
- How your code is being called, and
- What you are trying to assert.

3. Write minimally passing tests

Tests that include more information than is required to pass the test have a higher chance of introducing errors and can make the intent of the test less clear. For example, setting extra properties on models or using non-zero values when they are not required, only detracts from what you are trying to prove.

When writing unit tests, you want to focus on the behavior. To do this, the input that you use should be as simple as possible.

4. Avoid logic in tests

When you introduce logic into your test suite, the chance of introducing a bug through human error or false results increases dramatically. The last place that you want to find a bug is within your test suite because you should have a high level of confidence that your tests work. Otherwise, you will not trust them, and they do not provide any value.

When writing your unit tests, avoid manual string concatenation and logical conditions such as if, while, for, or switch, because this will help you avoid unnecessary logic.

5. Prefer helper methods for Setup and Teardown

In unit testing frameworks, a Setup function is called before each unit test within your test suite. Each test will generally have different requirements in order to get the test up and running. Unfortunately, Setup forces you to use the exact same requirements for each test. While some may see this as a useful tool, it generally ends up leading to bloated and hard-to-read tests. If you require a similar object or state for your tests, rather use an existing helper method than leverage Setup and Teardown attributes.

This will help by introducing:

- Less confusion when reading the tests since all of the code is visible from within each test.

- Less chance of setting up too much or too little for the given test.
- Less chance of sharing states between tests which would otherwise create unwanted dependencies between them.

6. Avoid multiple asserts

When introducing multiple asserts into a test case, it is not guaranteed that all of them will be executed. This is because the test will likely fail at the end of an earlier assertion, leaving the rest of the tests unexecuted. Once an assertion fails in a unit test, the proceeding tests are automatically considered to be failing, even if they are not. The result of this is then that the location of the failure is unclear, which also wastes debugging time.

When writing your tests, try to only include one assert per test. This helps to ensure that it is easy to pinpoint exactly what failed and why.

Like with all things coding related, knowing the theory is not enough and it requires practice to get good and build a habit, so these unit testing practices will take time to get right and feel neutral. The skill of writing a proper unit test though is incredibly undervalued and one that will add a lot of value to the quality of the code, so the effort and extra effort required is certainly worth it.

Static Analysis Techniques

Having defined best practices to build systems with is one thing. But no matter how well-intentioned we may be, there is no doubt that even the best developers are going to miss these principles from time to time. This is where a review process like Static Analysis comes in and can help to ensure that the software standards are maintained.

Yes, you could argue that unit tests should ensure the code is functioning, but they will only ensure that the code is functioning correctly. With various other security or performance tests covering some of the other important non-functional criteria in your software. These all cover aspects of the code that can be determined in its execution. But there are many aspects of code that are simply never executed or visible during the functional execution of a code that can still cause big quality concerns. And this is where static analysis comes in, as it evaluates the code without needing to execute it.

Some of the things that static analysis helps to uncover include:

Undefined or unused Values – Most compilers and IDEs should generally identify these values that have been declared and not used or not defined correctly, but sometimes these can be missed. Or, often crucially, be correctly used and defined, but in a piece of code that never gets executed or may cause violations when used in extreme circumstances that are not part of the unit tests.

160

Unused or undefined values might sound like something inconsequential if it doesn't affect the overall functionality of the software. However, it may cause dependency or maintenance issues over time when aspects of this code may become obsolete or incompatible with other systems. Any compiled code also adds to the overall size of the final deployment and this needs to be factored in.

Coding Standard Violations – We've spoken about the maintainability of code and the benefit that certain good practices have on a software's long-term viability. These issues can only be picked up through proper static analysis and linting rules. It's important that the clear guidelines that an organization sets out for its code are strictly adhered to and checked in this process.

Syntax Violations – Something which the majority of compilers should pick up, but tooling can be expanded to identify where these were missed or even identify the most obscure references that could cause a problem.

Security Vulnerabilities – We've already spoken about security tooling and most static analysis tools should provide for this and identify many of the predefined security rules and alert developers to them when their code does not adhere to these standards. And even if you are not utilizing a comprehensive security scanning tool, just setting up your static analysis tooling to search for the same things should make a significant difference

Memory Issues – Code that is not well optimized for memory usage will cause potential performance or functional issues and even system crashes in the case of buffer overflow

161

errors. The way software handles its different forms of memory is different to test for functionally, with even many performance tests unable to stress code enough to potentially identify the long-term effects of it. Having static scanning in place will help to identify the different issues in your memory declarations and usage and potentially save a lot of future issues.

The Benefit of Tooling

A lot of this analysis is not something that needs to be done manually. In the past, there were many forms of white-box testing techniques which could help developers and testers in the code review process to identify these certain patterns and get them fixed. A process that was incredibly time-intensive and so fraught with human error that it often didn't provide enough reward for all the labor to be suitably justifiable for companies to bother with it.

Thankfully, with scanning tools they can easily be run at a code repository layer and provide companies with meaningful reports of where issues in the code are and also trend to identify organizational methods of improvement, companies can utilize the static analysis process to incredible benefit and learn a lot about how they code in the process as the coding patterns can be analyzed too.

Scanning tools can also provide the added benefit of ensuring that all code is scanned and reviewed for some measure of quality. Whereas your unit tests will only test what you have designed for it to test and can only test parts of the code that are executable – these tools can ensure that all parts of the code are read and will have some measure of conformity and quality built into it.

They can also be executed incredibly quickly and obviously are not prone to human error, providing thorough and consistent results.

So, we should get rid of code reviews then?

With tools and tests that can essentially check everything in our code, does that mean that companies should do away with any formal code review process then? Well, not exactly. There are still some limitations to static analysis scanning and benefits to ensuring we always get a human eye on our code.

For a start, the following are limitations to static analysis tooling:

- False positives can be detected.
- A tool might not indicate what the defect is if there is a defect in the code.
- Not all coding rules can always be followed, like rules that need external documentation.
- Static analysis can't detect how a function will execute.
- System and third-party libraries may not be able to be analyzed.

However, despite these concerns, static analysis will still save a lot of time in covering the entire code and its finding can then be looked at in the code review process, where developers can both discuss its results and determine if changes need to be made. And also learn from it in the process as they better evaluate the logic of the code and see how certain parts of their coding can be executed better.

And it's that learning process that is perhaps the main reason why I would always adhere to a code review process. It's not just about saving time but helping developers to learn from one another will only have lasting benefits for any organization and provide a big boost to both the quality of their work and their development speed, as they will get better at delivering quality code the first time.

Types of static analysis
Most analysis tools may be automated and do the work for us, but it's still important to understand the type of work they do and how the different analysis done by these tools helps our software quality:

- **Control analysis** - focuses on the control flow in a calling structure. For example, a control flow could be a process, function, method, or subroutine.
- **Data analysis** - makes sure defined data is properly used while also making sure data objects are properly operating.
- **Fault/failure analysis** - analyzes faults and failures in model components.
- **Interface analysis** - verifies simulations to check the code and makes sure the interface fits into the model and simulation.

In a broader sense, with less official categorization, static analysis can be broken into formal, cosmetic, design properties, error checking, and predictive categories. Formal meaning if the code is correct; cosmetic meaning if the code syncs up with style standards; design properties meaning the level of complexities; error checking which looks for code violations; and predictive, which asks how code will behave when run.

Mutation Testing

Another common static testing approach that can be extremely valuable to any development team is mutation testing. Along with effective unit tests, mutation testing can provide one of the best forms of testing that can help to ensure quality at a code level.

Mutation testing often doesn't get too much attention drawn to it compared to many of the other forms of testing. And this is perhaps largely because mutation testing doesn't focus on the core functionality of the software, nor does it target any of the non-functional requirements that often form most of the focus of our quality. What it does do though, is help to identify the gaps in our unit testing approach and ensure that all-important decisions that the software needs to make, are catered for.

What is Mutation Testing

As the name suggests, mutation testing is a software testing type that is based on changes or mutations. Unlike regular testing which tests the source code as it is written, mutation testing rather introduces minuscule changes into the source code to check whether the defined test cases can detect errors in the code.

This adds an extra degree of test coverage to the unit testing effort, as it checks to verify that tests are correctly failing for changes in the code that should force the failure. This will not only test the effectiveness of the existing tests but also help the developers to write additional tests as it will help identify areas of code that their unit tests do not effectively cover.

Mutation testing derives its name from the mutations it brings to the code, which are effectively called mutants. The ideal case is that none of the test cases should pass. If the test passes, then it means that there is an error in the test code or a missing permutation. In mutation testing, this is referred to as a mutant. If the test fails, then there is no error in the code, and the mutant was killed. The goal of this testing is to kill all mutants.

It might seem a little strange to include mutation testing in a chapter on static analysis. However, even if the testing approach doesn't best conform to the definition of static analysis because code is executed − its purpose is to help improve the code and test coverage at a development level and forms part of a typical developer process. It is best done alongside the other static analysis techniques, and this is why I have placed it in this chapter. This form of testing can be done elsewhere, but it loses its value when done outside of the typical development process.

Mutation Testing Concepts

As mutation testing makes use of some rather unique terms, it's important to perhaps explain them in more detail so that you don't get confused.

#1) Mutants: Each time a change is made to the code, it forms a new mutant version of the code. When the test data is run through the mutant, it should ideally give us different results from the original source code. Mutants are also called **mutant programs**.

There are different types of mutants.

Survived Mutants: These are the mutants that are still alive after running test data through the original and mutated variants of the source code. These should be eliminated in your testing. They are also known as live mutants.

Killed Mutants: These are mutants that are killed after mutation testing. We get these when we get different results from the original and mutated versions of the source code.

Equivalent Mutants: These are closely related to live mutants, in that, they are 'alive' even after running test data through them. What differentiates them from others is that they have the same meaning as the original source code, even though they may have different syntax.

Mutators/mutation operators: These are what make mutations possible. I've already spoken about the importance of code coverage and ensuring that every decision made by your code is adequately tested. These operators or decision paths are what is changed in the mutation testing process. They can be referred to as faults or mutation rules.

Mutation score: This is a score that is calculated based on the number of mutants that have been identified and subsequently eliminated:

$$\text{Mutation score} = \frac{\text{Number of killed mutants}}{\text{Total number of mutants (survived and killed)}} * 100\%$$

In this calculation, equivalent mutants are not considered when calculating the mutation score. With the goal to ensure all mutants are successively eliminated the goal is to get as high a score as possible.

How To Do Mutation Testing

Well, now that we understand a few specifics about mutation testing, it's time to briefly discuss how it works. It might perhaps already be obvious that the mutation testing application will change operators in the code and verify that a test fails and catches the change – but to perhaps make the point clearer, I will illustrate it with the following actual example:

We will start with a Unit Test and an actual piece of code and then show how the code will undergo mutations to expose the lack of test coverage:

Unit Test

```
describe("User", function() {
        it("should compare the two numbers from user
        input", function(){
        expect(20).toBeGreaterThan(5);
```

```
        {}
{};
```

This unit test is a simple test to compare two numbers and ensure that the code can correctly identify that one is bigger than the other. In this case, that 20 is greater than 5.

Below is the actual code that is called by the test. In it, we enter two numbers, and it checks to see if the first number is lower than the second d and if it isn't, we will notify of the error and request the user to enter a second number value that is higher.

Original code (JavaScript)

```
const number_compare = () => {
   first_num = parseInt(prompt("Enter first number"))
   second_num = parseInt(prompt("Enter second number that
is higher than first number"))

   if (first_num < second_num) {
      alert(`Second number is ${second_num}. First number is
      ${first_num}.`)
      } else {
         alert(`Second number: ${second_num}, is more than
         first number: ${first_num}.
         Please enter the correct number`)
      }
}
number_compare();
```

Now, when we run this simple unit test, the outcome should be quite straightforward in that it will compare the two numbers and ensure that one is bigger than the other.

What mutation will do is focus on the operator in the code and switch it. Therefore changing the **greater-than** operator (first_num > second_num) to a **lesser than** operator (first_num < second_num)

This change will now change the result of the unit test with the number no longer being lower as expected – meaning the test will fail. This is the correct outcome and shows that in a function that in a small function like this, our simple test will provide the right amount of coverage.

Mutation Testing types

As with all forms of testing mutation testing also has multiple testing types that each serve a purpose:

Value Mutation

Here, we introduce a mutation by changing the parameter and/or constant values, usually by +/- 1.

Example: Original code (JavaScript)

```javascript
let arr = [2,3,4,5]
  for(let i=0; i<= 6;  i++){
        if(i%2===0){
        console.log(i*2)
    }
}
```

If the above code was meant to multiply the even numbers where **i<4**, then value mutation would mean changing the initialization to **let i=1**.

Statement Mutation

Here, we delete or duplicate a statement in a code block. We could also rearrange statements in a code block.

In an if-else block, for example, we could delete the else part or even the entire if-else block. So, if we take the duplication idea, the above code will look as follows:

Example: Original code (JavaScript)

```
let arr = [2,3,4,5]
  for(let i=0; i<= 6; i++){
        if(i%2===0){
        console.log(i*2)
        console.log(i*2)
    }
}
```

Decision Mutation

This is perhaps the most immediately identifiable type of mutation, where the operators are changed to provide different meanings – and thereby forcing the logic of a test to break accordingly.

Other operators that we can switch include the following:

Original operator	Mutant operator
<=	>=
>=	==

===	==
and	Or
||	&&

Mutation Testing Tools

This is not something that can be simply done with any self-built testing tool and so it's useful to make use of existing testing tools that can help with the mutation testing approach. While not an exhaustive list, tools like Stryker, Jumble, PIT, and Insure++ are all recommended and capable of performing mutation testing across a wide number of programming languages.

Why Mutation Testing

Hopefully, you can already see the immense value that mutation testing can bring in improving the quality of the code and unit test approach. As with other static analysis approaches, it covers a large portion of your code that may be missed by other functional testing techniques. It also tests specific parts of the code and not just paths, branches, or statements. Allowing for more completeness in the testing effort than would otherwise be considered by typical test analysis.

The caveats to Mutation testing

However, there are risks and the primary issue with mutation testing is that it is incredibly resource-intensive. Each code mutation takes time to process and compile, plus the unit tests then need to be executed in the process. Do this for each possible permutation in a line of code and you can easily see how this adds up in both the cost of computing resources and time.

For this reason, I strongly recommend that mutation testing is not conducted in a testing pipeline like other forms of testing, but rather – again – forms part of a code review and static analysis process. Mutation testing is also best conducted on a local machine so that any form of shared infrastructure or cloud computing is not utilized, as this would prove incredibly expensive for a company.

This should not detract from the use of mutation testing and even if it adds a considerable amount of time to the testing at a code and unit level, the improvement to the overall code quality makes up for it and a software development team will make this up with a reduced testing effort at a component and end-to-end level if all parts of the code have gone through this process effectively.

Reviewing your code improves your code

At the end of the day, one of the biggest benefits that all forms of static analysis bring is that it helps developers to improve their coding abilities. If companies are serious about training and improving the skills of their development team, then enforcing processes around static analysis and mutation testing will allow them to do just that, while also allowing them to be productive and deliver better quality software.

Designing for Security

With the constant threat of security faced in the modern software world where malicious players will look to expose any vulnerabilities they can to either steal or expose sensitive information or try and disrupt your service, it is imperative when designing software that we look to mitigate these issues as early as possible. Trying to identify and fix security gaps too late in the development process can prove expensive as many of the biggest vulnerabilities arise from poor design and require significant effort to fix. Using up time that could have easily been prevented if the right principles were followed in the design phase.

To ensure your software is ready to meet these rigorous security demands, it needs to meet the following principles:

Confidentiality: Only authorized people (or processes) can get access.
Integrity: The presented data is unaltered.
Availability: The system and its data are available even under adverse circumstances.
Authenticity: Users are whom they claim to be.

These security criteria should be something that becomes embedded into the operation of the company and not just security guidelines that come when code is written. This needs to form part of the functional requirements of the software and how things get designed from the very beginning. If requirements do not cater to a functional way of how confidentiality will be handled across every part of a software system, then even developers coding in a very secure manner is unlikely to resolve the issues.

Before we get into the different principles that need to be followed, it's important to get your processes aligned and ensure that your business, architecture, developers, and other stakeholders are all aligned in ensuring that secure design is not compromised at any point of the development journey.

Developing use/misuse cases

Work with the architecture group to model use and misuse cases. While use cases depict the application's functionality, the inverse of the use cases (misuse cases) is modeled to understand and address the software design's security aspects. These are known things in the way software can be misused to expose or exploit vulnerabilities. These misuse cases should be turned into standard case templates that can be used to form the basis of security testing and security scans and ensure that the software requirements take all these cases into consideration.

Performing software security design and architecture reviews

The security architect should get involved when the teams are engaged in the functional design and architecture review of the software. To ease this process, try using the checklist approach since that works great and can be tracked. It is imperative that the architects in charge of security work closely with the architecture team to generate a software security plan which outlines its design in detail. The same can

175

be used as a check-and-balance guide during and after development.

Performing threat and risk modeling

Threat modeling helps in determining the software's attack surface by examining its functionality for trust boundaries, entry points, data flows, and exit points. If you are not familiar with the technique, use a threat modeling tool, because it always comes in handy for this exercise. The next activity that follows is the risk modeling of software. It is accomplished by ranking the threats as they pertain to the organization's business objectives, compliance and regulatory requirements, and security exposures.

These can be rather lengthy processes for companies to perform and may come with measures that could easily frustrate many of the development team as certain restrictions may seemingly take their freedom away. However, when you consider the costs that security vulnerabilities cost a company, its reputation, and importantly, its customers, then it should be seen as a necessity despite the potential disruption.

Generating test cases

Try and use a combination of misuse cases, security design, and architecture reviews, as well as threat and risk modeling, to generate a detailed security requirements document (technical details), which the developers can then use to write code. You can also use this plan to generate security test cases that should be executed during testing. Using a scenario-based security testing template is effective in ensuring that the bare minimum security test cases are performed in every software development effort.

Guiding

While performing the above tasks, take some time to document them and build certain measures into your security tooling, because they can serve as guidance or knowledge base. Document the best practices for secure architecture and design, review checklists, and design considerations, which can be used as standard guidance tools organization-wide. These are living documents that get updated with changes in technology. Good practice calls for documenting design decisions made for security reasons, as well as ensuring traceability of design items and decisions to requirements and code. Traceability is essential for the assurance case.

As you start to build these practices into your organization, there should be a change in culture where security is taken more seriously. When you have the support of an organization, it is then easier to ensure that the following principles are designed into the software to provide it with the needed security. Not all of these are principles that relate to pure coding or software development, but also represent certain system rules that need to be in place to govern the behavior of the software in a secure way.

As I say this though it is worth mentioning a caveat that there is no single silver bullet when it comes to software security and while these principles should all go a long way in mitigating a software system from the threats of security vulnerabilities and attacks, the threats faced are changing on a regular basis and so it's important that companies never take their security for granted and keep revising their testing and development procedures to stay abreast of any potential security threats.

Least Privilege Design Principle

The general rule behind this principle is to provide the least amount of access privileges that any individual needs. Often, in err of trying to become more efficient, companies tend to give people too much access to allow them to do their jobs.

The implications of granting access beyond this scope will allow for unnecessary access and the potential for data to be updated out of the approved context. The assigning of access rights will limit system-damaging attacks from users whether they are intentional or not.

This principle attempts to limit data changes and prevents potential damage from occurring by accident or error by reducing the number of potential interactions with a resource.

This is not just true for human users but also for system-generated accounts. System accounts that the software will use to interact with various other components or infrastructure in a system should only have the access to interact with the systems it needs and perform the tasks required. This way, even if the code does something unintended or it gets compromised in some way, there is a limit to how much it can damage the rest of the system.

Fail-Safe Defaults Design Principle

This principle goes hand-in-hand with the principle of least privilege. The Fail-Safe Defaults design principle pertains to allowing access to resources based on granted access over access exclusion. This means that any access is granted only if explicitly needed and that by default, users do not have access to any resources until the access has been granted

This prevents unauthorized users from gaining access to any resources unless explicitly authorized to do so.

Economy of Mechanism Design Principle

You are probably picking up a trend around the concept of simplicity in many of the design aspects in this book, but it just goes to show how important simplicity is to building a safe and secure software system.

The Economy of Mechanism design principle requires that systems should be designed as simple and small as possible. As we've already learned, simple code is easy to test and this applies to security as well, as the different security scanning and security tests will be easier to write if the code is small and uncomplex.

Added complexity increases the likelihood of testing scenarios being missed and also certain faults in the code going unnoticed.

Open Design Principle

The Open Design Principle is the concept that the security of a system and its algorithms should not be dependent on the secrecy of its design or implementation.

This is an important principle for the open-source movement that the software world is currently in. While companies want to protect their intellectual property and may want to therefore not provide others access to their code, the reason should never be for security reasons. If there is an aspect of your code that you feels exposes your security in any way, then it probably should be redesigned.

Putting scanning software in place should help to identify any issues like this in the code, but it also requires a bigger look at how systems interact with the code and for teams to actively review the code and test for these areas.

Separation Privilege Design Principle

The separation privilege design principle requires that all approved resources access attempts be granted based on more than a single condition. For example, a user should be validated for active status and have access to that specific resource.

Doing this sounds like an extra system administration overhead as it makes access more difficult, but this added measure can provide a lot of additional protection to ensure any users or resources do not behave in unexpected ways.

Least Common Mechanism Design Principle

The Least Common Mechanism design principle declares that mechanisms used to access resources should not be shared.

So, this is another principle that requires additional overhead and effort to develop more mechanisms that handle the different permissions management and access of resources, but in separating these areas, it reduces the risk should any system become compromised or perform incorrectly in any way.

Defense in Depth Design Principle

The Defense in Depth design principle is a concept of layering resource access authorization verification in a system that reduces the chance of a successful attack. This layered approach to resource authorization requires unauthorized users to circumvent each authorization attempt to gain access to a resource.

When designing a system that requires meeting a security quality attribute architects need to consider the scope of security needs and the minimum required security qualities.

Not every system will need to use all of the basic security design principles but will use one or more in combination based on its threshold for system security because the existence of security in an application adds an additional layer to the overall system and can affect performance.

That is why the definition of minimum security acceptably is needed when a system is designed because these quality attributes need to be factored in with the other system quality attributes so that the system in question adheres to all qualities based on the priorities of the qualities.

Secure Coding

So, the principles from the previous chapter should make a drastic impact in enforcing the security of our systems if we can apply them correctly. However, we still need to write the code that needs to wrap around these principles and that too requires a lot of deliberate effort.

Yes, there are a lot of automated scans that can be used to help with this that will highlight all the areas of code that are at risk and can give you an opportunity to then change it. However, it is important that you don't just rely on scanning – though please do implement these scans – and understand things to watch out for and why so that you can design the code securely from the start and not just fix it retrospectively as you go along.

So, hopefully, the below tips will prove helpful to you in building code that can meet the strictest of security measures.

General Coding Practices
Regardless of the type of programming you are doing, the following principles are useful to implement in your coding practices:

- Use tested and approved managed code rather than creating new unmanaged code for common tasks.
- Utilize task-specific built-in APIs to conduct operating system tasks. Do not allow the application to issue commands directly to the Operating System,

especially through the use of application-initiated command shells.

- Use checksums or hashes to verify the integrity of interpreted code, libraries, executables, and configuration files.
- Utilize locking to prevent multiple simultaneous requests or use a synchronization mechanism to prevent race conditions.
- Protect shared variables and resources from inappropriate concurrent access.
- Explicitly initialize all your variables and other data stores, either during declaration or just before the first usage.
- Avoid calculation errors by understanding your programming language's underlying representation and how it interacts with numeric calculation. Pay close attention to byte size discrepancies, precision, signed/unsigned distinctions, truncation, conversion, and casting between types, "not-a-number" calculations, and how your language handles numbers that are too large or too small for its underlying representation.
- Do not pass user-supplied data to any dynamic execution function.
- Implement safe updating. If the application will utilize automatic updates, then use cryptographic signatures for your code and ensure your download clients verify those signatures. Use encrypted channels to transfer the code from the host server

Input Validation

Most of the areas where your code is most exposed to malicious threats is the area of user input. Whether it be code or SQL injections, malicious actors will do their best to try and expose sensitive information through your application's different input methods.

Centralize your input validation

Create a centralized input validation routine for the application, so that your security can be streamlined and standardized across the application. It also allows your security professionals to test one area, streamlining the security testing process.

Within this one program you can now include all the important mechanisms that will help to ensure all user input is sufficiently validated:

- Specify proper character sets, such as UTF-8, for all sources of input
- Encode data to a common character set before validating (Canonicalize).
- All validation failures should result in input rejection.
- Validate all client-provided data before processing, including all parameters, URLs, and HTTP header content (e.g., Cookie names and values). Be sure to include automated postbacks from JavaScript, Flash, or other embedded code
- Verify that header values in both requests and responses contain only ASCII characters.
- Validate data from redirects. An attacker may submit malicious content directly to the target of the

redirect, thus circumventing application logic and any validation performed before the redirect

- Validate for expected data types.
- Check for null bytes (%00)
- Check for new line characters (%0d, %0a, \r, \n)
- Check for "dot-dot-slash" (../ or ..\) path alterations characters or in cases where UTF-8 extended character set encoding is supported, address alternate representation like: %c0%ae%c0%ae/ (Utilize canonicalization to address double encoding or other forms of obfuscation attacks)

Output Encoding

Output Encoding is a process where you translate special characters into a different, but equivalent, form so that they will not be read as malicious code by any part of the software system.

Any potentially hazardous characters must be allowed as input, be sure that you implement additional controls like output encoding, secure task-specific APIs, and accounting for the utilization of that data throughout the application. Examples of common hazardous characters include: < > " ' % () & + \ \' \"

- Contextually output and encode all data returned to the client that originated outside the application's trust boundary. HTML entity encoding is one example but does not work in all cases.
- Encode all characters unless they are known to be safe for the intended interpreter.

- Contextually sanitize all output of un-trusted data to queries for SQL, XML, and LDAP.
- Sanitize all output of un-trusted data to operating system commands.

Authentication and Password Management

Along with user input, authentication, and password management is another critical area that malicious actors like to focus on. Any vulnerabilities in your authentication process may allow these actors to gain access to a system that they should not have access to.

Similarly, you do not want passwords, the most critical information that allows users to access your system to be exposed in any way – so you want to ensure that you adhere to the best practices to prevent this from ever happening.

- Like with input validation, use a centralized implementation for all authentication controls, including libraries that call external authentication services
- Establish and utilize standard, tested, authentication services whenever possible. There is no point in trying to create these important security mechanisms on your own when many excellent options already exist. And this is one area where you don't want to skimp on, so pay those licensing fees, if required.
- Segregate authentication logic from the resource being requested and use redirection to and from the centralized authentication control.
- If your application manages a credential store, it should ensure that only cryptographically strong one-

way salted hashes of passwords are stored and that the table/file that stores the passwords and keys is writeable only by the application. (Do not use the MD5 algorithm if it can be avoided).

- Validate the authentication data only on completion of all data input, especially for sequential authentication implementations.
- Authentication failure responses should not indicate which part of the authentication data was incorrect. For example, instead of "Invalid username" or "Invalid password", just use "Invalid username and/or password" for both. Error responses must be truly identical in both display and source code.
- Utilize authentication for connections to external systems that involve sensitive information or functions.
- Authentication credentials for accessing services external to the application should be encrypted and stored in a protected location on a trusted system. The source code is NOT a secure location.
- Use only HTTP POST requests to transmit authentication credentials.
- Only send non-temporary passwords over an encrypted connection or as encrypted data, such as in an encrypted email. Temporary passwords associated with email resets may be an exception.
- Enforce password complexity requirements established by policy or regulation. Authentication credentials should be sufficient to withstand attacks that are typical of the threats in the deployed

environment. (e.g., requiring the use of alphabetic as well as numeric and/or special characters).

- Enforce account disabling after an established number of invalid login attempts (e.g., five attempts is common). The account must be disabled for a period of time sufficient to discourage brute force guessing of credentials, but not so long as to allow for a denial-of-service attack to be performed.
- Password rules and reset mechanisms should meet whatever is required by the organization. Critical systems should have strict rules with regular changes and 2FA, whereas non-critical accounts do not need to require frequent password changes.
- The last use (successful or unsuccessful) of a user account should be reported to the user at their next successful login.
- Implement monitoring to identify attacks against multiple user accounts, utilizing the same password. This attack pattern is used to bypass standard lockouts when user IDs can be harvested or guessed.
- Change all vendor-supplied default passwords and user IDs or disable the associated accounts.
- Re-authenticate users prior to performing critical operations.
- Use Multi-Factor Authentication for highly sensitive or high-value transactional accounts.
- If using third-party code for authentication, inspect the code carefully to ensure it is not affected by any malicious code.
-

Session Management

Users require authentication, but with a lot of other services operating in the background that all need to interact with that user and therefore need to know who they are, session management also becomes crucial to ensure a user remains authenticated across the system, without their access token becoming compromised in any way by malicious parties.

The following guidelines are worth following to ensure secure session management in any application:

- Session identifier creation must always be done on a trusted system (some internal server or secure application) with only these tokens accepted across the system.
- Use a single site-wide component to check access authorization. This includes libraries that call external authorization services.
- Set the domain and path for cookies containing authenticated session identifiers to an appropriately restricted value for the site.
- Segregate privileged logic from other application code
- Logout functionality should fully terminate the associated session or connection and be available from all pages protected by authorization.
- Establish a session inactivity timeout that is as short as possible, based on balancing risk and business functional requirements. In most cases, it should be no more than several hours.

- Disallow persistent logins and enforce periodic session terminations, even when the session is active. Especially for applications supporting rich network connections or connecting to critical systems. Termination times should support business requirements and the user should receive sufficient notification to mitigate negative impacts.
- If a session was established before login, close that session and establish a new session after a successful login with the generation of a new session identifier on any re-authentication.
- Limit the number of transactions a single user or device can perform in a given period of time before re-authentication is required. The transactions/time should be above the actual business requirement, but low enough to deter automated attacks.
- Do not allow concurrent logins with the same user ID.
- Do not expose session identifiers in URLs, error messages, or logs. Session identifiers should only be in the HTTP cookie header. For example, do not pass session identifiers as GET parameters.
- Protect server-side session data from unauthorized access, by other users of the server, by implementing appropriate access controls on the server.
- Generate a new session identifier and deactivate the old one periodically. (This can mitigate certain session hijacking scenarios where the original identifier was compromised).

- Supplement standard session management for sensitive server-side operations, like account management, by utilizing per-session strong random tokens or parameters. This method can be used to prevent Cross-Site Request Forgery attacks.
- Supplement standard session management for highly sensitive or critical operations by utilizing per-request, as opposed to per-session, strong random tokens, or parameters.
- Set the "secure" attribute for cookies transmitted over a TLS connection.
- Set cookies with the HTTP Only attribute unless you specifically require client-side scripts within your application to read or set a cookie's value.
- Try and avoid using any form of state data to capture information about the user session, though if state data must be stored on the client, use encryption and integrity checking on the server side to catch state tampering.
- All cryptographic functions used to protect secrets from the application user must be implemented on a trusted system.
- All random numbers, random file names, random GUIDs, and random strings should be generated using the cryptographic module's approved random number generator when these random values are intended to be un-guessable.
- Cryptographic modules used by the application should be compliant with FIPS 140-2 or an equivalent standard.

Error Handling and Logging

Errors happen and it's important that our system gathers as much information about how and why they occur to ensure they are properly fixed in the future. At the same time, you want to log various aspects of usage on the site to better understand user behavior and understand what is happening on the site.

Capturing this information correctly and securely though is a challenge and so the following measures need to be included to allow your application to do so:

- Do not disclose sensitive information in error responses, including system details, session identifiers, or account information. Similarly, do not store sensitive information in logs, including unnecessary system details, session identifiers, or passwords.
- Use error handlers that do not display debugging or stack trace information.
- Implement generic error messages and use custom error pages.
- The application should handle application errors and not rely on the server configuration.
- Free allocated memory when error conditions occur
- Error handling logic associated with security controls should deny access by default.
- Logging controls should support both success and failure of specified security events
- Ensure logs contain important log event data.

- Ensure log entries that include un-trusted data will not execute as code in the intended log viewing interface or software.
- Restrict access to logs to only authorized individuals.
- Utilize a master routine for all logging operations
- Ensure that a mechanism exists to conduct log analysis.
- Log all input validation failures, access control failures, authentication attempts (including failures), tampering events, unexpected changes in state data or any token or connection failures to any part of the system.
- Use a cryptographic hash function to validate log entry integrity.

Data Protection

Along with all the above measures, we need to ensure that any personal or sensitive data is stored securely and cannot be intercepted either at rest or in transit between different parts of the system.

- Protect all cached or temporary copies of sensitive data stored on the server from unauthorized access and purge those temporary working files as soon as they are no longer required.
- Encrypt highly sensitive stored information, like authentication verification data, even on the server side.
- Protect server-side source code from being downloaded by a user.

- Do not store passwords, connection strings, or other sensitive information in clear text or in any Non cryptographically secure manner on the client side.
- Remove comments in user-accessible production code that may reveal backend system or other sensitive information
- Remove unnecessary application and system documentation as this can reveal useful information to attackers
- Do not include sensitive information in HTTP GET request parameters
- Disable client-side caching on pages containing sensitive information. Cache-Control: no-store, may be used in conjunction with the HTTP header control "Pragma: no-cache", which is less effective, but is HTTP/1.0 backward compatible
- The application should support the removal of sensitive data when that data is no longer required. (e.g. personal information or certain financial data)
- Implement appropriate access controls for sensitive data stored on the server. This includes cached data, temporary files, and data that should be accessible only by specific system users.

Communication Security

Systems will need to communicate with one another and while much of this should be done through secure channels and protected by various firewalls within a secure network, it's still important as develops to also build certain communication protocols into all of our intra-application communication:

- Implement encryption for the transmission of all sensitive information. This should include TLS for protecting the connection and may be supplemented by discrete encryption of sensitive files or non-HTTP based connections
- TLS certificates should be valid and have the correct domain name, not be expired, and be installed with intermediate certificates when required
- Failed TLS connections should not fall back to an insecure connection.
- Utilize TLS connections for all content requiring authenticated access and for all other sensitive information.
- Utilize TLS for connections to external systems that involve sensitive information or functions.
- Utilize a single standard TLS implementation that is configured appropriately.
- Specify character encodings for all connections
- Filter parameters containing sensitive information from the HTTP referrer, when linking to external sites.

System Configuration

While this may not traditionally be seen as something within the realm of programming, within a DevOps world where developers are increasingly controlling system configurations systems through code, it's important that all developers learn how to implement secure system configurations across all servers, virtual machines ad containers operating application software:

Secure Coding

- Ensure servers, frameworks, and system components are running the latest approved version and have all patches issued for the version in use
- Turn off directory listings
- Restrict the web server, process, and service accounts to the least privileges possible.
- Remove all unnecessary functionality and files.
- Ensure any test code or any other code not required for production operation is not part of the deployment scripts.
- Prevent disclosure of your directory structure in the robots.txt file by placing directories not intended for public indexing into an isolated parent directory. Then "Disallow" that entire parent directory in the robots.txt file rather than disallowing each individual directory
- Define which HTTP methods, Get or Post, the application will support and whether it will be handled differently on different pages in the application.
- Disable unnecessary HTTP methods, such as WebDAV extensions. If an extended HTTP method that supports file handling is required, utilize a well-vetted authentication mechanism.
- Remove unnecessary information from HTTP response headers related to the OS, web-server version, and application frameworks.
- The security configuration store for the application should be able to be output in human-readable form to support auditing.

- Implement an asset management system and register system components and software in it.
- Isolate development environments from the production network and provide access only to authorized development and test groups. Development environments are often configured less securely than production environments and attackers may use this difference to discover shared weaknesses or as an avenue for exploitation.
- Implement a software change control system to manage and record changes to the code both in development and production.

Database Security

As the place where we store all of our valuable data, a database is a place that needs a lot of security. Much of which the developer can control. And even if your architecture is not using a traditional database to focus more on other NoSQL or Blockchain platforms, some of these points may still be incredibly useful to you too:

- Use strongly typed parameterized queries that use variables that are strongly typed. This enforces strict restrictions on different data types and prevents certain data types from being used incorrectly.
- Utilize input validation and output encoding and be sure to address meta characters.
- Connection strings should not be hard coded within the application. Connection strings should be stored in a separate configuration file on a trusted system, and they should be encrypted.

- Use stored procedures to abstract data access and allow for the removal of permissions to the base tables in the database.
- Close the connection as soon as possible.
- Turn off all unnecessary database functionality (e.g., unnecessary stored procedures or services, utility packages, install only the minimum set of features and options required (surface area reduction)).
- Remove unnecessary default vendor content (e.g., sample schemas).
- Disable any default accounts that are not required to support business requirements.
- The application should connect to the database with different credentials for every trust distinction (e.g., user, read-only user, guest, administrators).

File Management

Like databases, the way applications manage files has a big impact on protecting critical data and as such, it's important that we get this right. The following principles should help with the management of your applications file systems:

- Do not pass user-supplied data directly to any dynamic include function.
- Require authentication before allowing a file to be uploaded.
- Limit the type of files that can be uploaded to only those types that are needed for business purposes.
- Validate uploaded files are the expected type by checking file headers. Checking for file type by extension alone is not sufficient.

- Do not save files in the same web context as the application. Files should either go to the content server or in the database.
- Prevent or restrict the uploading of any file that may be interpreted by the web server.
- Turn off execution privileges on file upload directories
- Implement safe uploading in UNIX by mounting the targeted file directory as a logical drive using the associated path or the chrooted environment.
- When referencing existing files, use a whitelist of allowed file names and types. Validate the value of the parameter being passed and if it does not match one of the expected values, either reject it or use a hard-coded default file value for the content instead.
- Do not pass user-supplied data into a dynamic redirect. If this must be allowed, then the redirect should accept only validated, relative path URLs.
- Do not pass directory or file paths, use index values mapped to a pre-defined list of paths.
- Never send the absolute file path to the client.
- Ensure application files and resources are read-only.
- Scan user uploaded files for viruses and malware.

Memory Management

Lastly, we have memory management. How an application uses computer memory is critical, not just to its overall usage and performance, but also to security as critical information can be stored and interpreted in transit through a computer's memory and so it's important as developers that this is handled in a secure manner:

- Utilize input and output control for un-trusted data
- Double check that the buffer is as large as specified
- When using functions that accept a number of bytes to copy, such as strncpy(), be aware that if the destination buffer size is equal to the source buffer size, it may not NULL-terminate the string.
- Check buffer boundaries if calling the function in a loop and make sure there is no danger of writing past the allocated space.
- Truncate all input strings to a reasonable length before passing them to the copy and concatenation functions
- Specifically close resources don't rely on garbage collection. (e.g., connection objects, file handles, etc.)
- Use non-executable stacks when available
- Avoid the use of known vulnerable functions (e.g., printf, Strat, strcpy etc.)
- Properly free allocated memory upon the completion of functions and at all exit points.

There is a lot to think about when it comes to application security and these principles are not a complete list as there are many vulnerabilities and improvements to device security that are getting discovered every day. If we can work to design a software architecture around secure principles and implement our code with these same considerations in mind, it's likely that your software applications will be able to withstand many of the security threats that will come its way, both current and in the future.

How to approach Security Testing

With the world increasingly relying on software and the internet for just about anything, it only makes sense that security receives so much focus. After all, with so much critical data lying around, it is important that companies place heavy emphasis on security testing and the process of identifying their security flaws to ensure their software is safe.

The biggest issue with software security and the testing of it is the pace of change in the number and types of vulnerabilities. While there are ways, we can secure our code from a wide number of vulnerabilities and known detections, that doesn't mean that there aren't a variety of other potentials security holes that could come from any number of issues from third-party applications, browsers, operating systems, and networking systems that are often beyond your control. Still, conducting some of the testing methods below should help to ensure that you can detect all possible known security risks and fix these problems correctly during development.

One of the main reasons I have seen people stay clear of security testing is because they believe it is a very niche and highly expertise form of testing and thus leave it to the security professionals and ethical hackers out there to get involved in. And I personally vouch to always ensure that companies follow these forms of expertise, largely because security is not something you can compromise on. However, there is a lot that any tester or engineer can bring to the table in the security testing process, and the more regularly you test your security, the easier it is for security to be maintained even when delivering changes to software rapidly.

Types of Security Testing:

Mainstream entertainment may show hackers or security professionals as these highly sophisticated and cool coders, but the truth is that a lot of security testing and the ethical hacking components of it is a lot more reliant on using many tools and tricks to help find flaws rather than a result of some programmatic genius.

There are seven main types of security tests and assessments that you will need to be aware of and consider applying to your software system. Each topic can easily be delved into in more detail by security experts, however, I will admit that I am not one. It is important though to understand these all at a high level and know when and where to apply them to help ensure the correct security measures are in place in your software:

Vulnerability Scanning: This is done through automated software to scan a system against known vulnerability signatures. It will scan your code and look for parts of your code that are vulnerable to the likes of SQL or code injections, along with many other knowing vulnerabilities that may exist in certain packages.

Security Scanning: It involves identifying network and system weaknesses and identifying solutions for reducing these risks.

Much like vulnerability scanning, there are many tools available that can scan networks to identify these risks.

Penetration testing: This kind of testing simulates an attack from a malicious hacker. This testing involves the analysis of a particular system to check for potential vulnerabilities to an external hacking attempt. This differs from the traditional ethical hacking described later, as it reproduces a known approach and can be automated, rather than having a group of hackers looking to replicate and find flaws in a more exploratory manner.

Risk Assessment: Less a form of testing and more an evaluation of the different risks to help identify what needs to be prioritized and focused on most importantly. Risks are classified as Low, Medium, and High. These controls and measures are normally associated with each risk to help identify ways of mitigating it to further help an organization make the right decisions in tackling these security risks.

Security Auditing: This is an internal inspection of Applications and Operating systems for security flaws. An audit can also be done via a line-by-line inspection of code. It can seem painfully boring and cumbersome, but if you know what to look for, can be very effective.

Ethical hacking: It's hacking an Organization's Software system. Unlike malicious hackers, who steal for their own gains, the intent is to expose security flaws in the system. These flaws are then reported on and used to identify improvements in the software.

Posture Assessment: An extension of the risk assessment above. This combines Security scanning, Ethical Hacking, and Risk Assessments to show an overall security posture of an organization.

How to do Security Testing

Much like all other phases of software development, the earlier you can identify and prevent security flaws, the better. This shouldn't be something left to the end of a project. It's also something that teams should formulate a strategy for addressing and utilize various tools and approaches to help them identify security flaws through their development lifecycles and sprints.

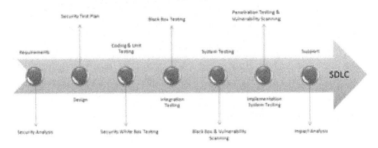

The above phases show the type of testing that should be conducted at each phase of a development lifecycle. This is obviously blurred in an agile and DevOps world, but the importance of covering all these aspects of testing is incredibly important.

Have a properly documented strategy

One of the things though that is very important when it comes to security testing that is often disregarded these days is that of a proper strategy. While people have forgone many aspects of documentation and rather built traceability through their various tools and worked in a more ad-hoc and flexible approach, with security you can't take chances, and as such you need to ensure that a proper strategy is developed, documented, and clearly implemented in the SDLC as above so that teams are clear when and how to test for vulnerabilities.

Having it properly documented and outlined also makes it easier from an auditing perspective, because that is one aspect of your development that auditors will latch on to and you want to ensure you have your bases covered here.

Any proper test strategy around security should include the following:

- Security-related test cases or scenarios
- Test Data related to security testing
- Test Tools required for security testing
- Analysis of various test outputs from different security tools

The reason for this multi-pronged approach is because software security is complex, but also something that you can't compromise on. You want to hit it in as many places as possible and as often as possible.

Included in your test strategy should not be a documented outline of approach, tools, and analysis, but often helpful to include specifics on which tests needed to be executed as a bare minimum outside of the default scans, to ensure that many basics are taken care of.

Examples of Test Scenarios for Security Testing:

Sample Test scenarios to give you a glimpse of security test cases -

- A password should be in an encrypted format
- Application or System should not allow invalid users
- Check cookies and session time for application
- For financial sites, the Browser back button should not work.

Methodologies/ Approach / Techniques for Security Testing

In security testing, different methodologies are followed, and they are as follows:

Tiger Box: This hacking is usually done on a laptop that has a collection of OSs and hacking tools. This testing helps penetration testers and security testers to conduct vulnerabilities assessment and attacks.

Black Box: The tester is authorized to do testing on everything about the network topology and the technology.

Grey Box: Partial information is given to the tester about the system, and it is a hybrid of white and black box models.

Security Testing Tools

Given the reliance on tools to be able to assess and detect security vulnerabilities effectively, it's important to have a look at some of the different tools available to help companies assess which will work for them.

1) Owasp

The Open Web Application Security Project (OWASP) is a worldwide non-profit organization focused on improving the security of software. The project has multiple tools to pen test various software environments and protocols. Flagship tools of the project include

- Zed Attack Proxy (ZAP – an integrated penetration testing tool)
- OWASP Dependency Check (It scans for project dependencies and checks against know vulnerabilities)
- OWASP Web Testing Environment Project (Collection of security tools and documentation)

2) WireShark

Wireshark is a network analysis tool previously known as Ethereal. It captures data packets in real-time and displays them in a human-readable format. Basically, it is a network packet analyzer - which provides the minute details about your network protocols, decryption, packet information, etc. It is open-source and can be used on Linux, Windows, OS X, Solaris, NetBSD, FreeBSD, and many other systems. The information that is retrieved via this tool can be viewed through a GUI or the TTY mode TShark Utility.

3) W3af

w3af is a web application attack and audit framework. It has three types of plugins; discovery, audit, and attack that communicate with each other for any vulnerabilities in the site, for example, a discovery plugin in w3af looks for different URLs to test for vulnerabilities and forward it to the audit plugin which then uses these URLs to search for vulnerabilities.

You can't compromise on the security of your software and therefore can't afford to compromise on the effectiveness of your thing strategy towards it. And it's not just for certain experts, but vital that every member of a team does their part in building a secure system.

Designing for Performance

Much like writing easily laid out and secure code, writing code that can execute optimally takes a lot of hard work and is often counterintuitive to how many of us would like to code. Often, we focus on the simplest way to solve a problem or the fastest/least number of lines in which code can be written. The challenge of trying to achieve the most optimal solutions however is a lot more daunting than many of us would want to take.

Thankfully, thinking in an optimal fashion can become a matter of habit the more often it is practiced and so while it will slow you down quite a lot at the start. The more you get used to thinking about efficient coding algorithms and putting tests in place to ensure the code is always at its most optimal, the faster you get at solving these challenges naturally.

Before I get into things to consider in coding for optimization though, it is perhaps worth saying that not everything needs to work ultra-fast. Sometimes you can be working on an API or application that will only get called every few hours or so, is internal facing, and doesn't impact the dependencies of other code. In cases such as this, often solving the problem as simply as possible is good enough. However, the majority of work that developers will do is likely to have some impact on the overall performance of a system and so learning how to optimize your code for performance is an important skill to   master.

As I get into the code-level details on things that can improve the speed of your code, I'm going to hit this topic in different ways. Firstly, give you some approaches and thoughts to think about when measuring the performance of your software. Second speak about some challenges around coding for performance and lastly, some tips to actually write more streamlined code.

Measuring your existing performance

It is difficult to know if your coding is optimized until you have a way of measuring it effectively and so it's important that we start with this.

Get the right metric

A lot of the problems covered above come from measuring the wrong things. You can be measuring server response time rather than the time it takes a web page to render. Or measure performance using specific datasets without those datasets necessarily being production specific.

Making sure you are measuring the right number is the single most important thing to do when tackling a performance problem. Without that, you have no idea how much you are helping. Similarly, don't necessarily trust those more experienced than you to tell you the bottleneck. Make sure you evaluate it yourself. I discuss some of these metrics in more detail in my chapter on Performance Testing later in the book.

Measure right

Lots of things can affect your performance measurement. You might be a mobile developer with a slick test device that has only one program running on it. If your goal is to produce a response in < 10ms on average, that will be a lot easier on your test device than on your user's four-year-old phone with a low battery and a hundred apps running in the background.

It could also cause you to misunderstand your program's characteristics. You might be I/O bound on a test device when on most devices you are actually CPU bound.

All sorts of external factors can affect performance including:

- Memory usage
- Server load
- Network bandwidth and latency
- Battery level
- CPU usage
- Disk usage
- Various caches at all layers
- OS or Web Browser Versioning

I unpack some of these factors a little more in my next chapter on performance testing where we look at how to measure some of these things (though not all, as it would prove too exhaustive for this book) in more detail.

When you're measuring, try to make sure as many factors as possible are held constant so you can accurately compare different approaches. But also make an effort to understand what these factors usually look like, so you can make sure your appraisal of bottlenecks is realistic.

Measure both prod and test environments

It makes sense that you want to measure how your software is performing in production, but you should also be doing this as part of your general development cycle as well in a proper dev environment. Performance monitoring is underrated in the development space. I understand that dev environment stability is sporadic and not always production-like and that it takes a lot of effort to put the necessary monitoring tools in place, but the value in catching things quickly outweighs that.

The biggest thing though is understanding that performance between your production and development environments are likely to be different and so you need to benchmark based on those differences. And if you have multiple development environments, each one should be benchmarked.

The reason for that is simple, each environment has a variety of its own environmental variables that affect performance, and you want a standard baseline in which to measure against. And while development environments are less reliable, you can still effectively measure the performance of your code. If you measure it regularly and often. That way, deviations can be easily picked up and whether it is code, DB or environmental related will also be a lot easier to determine.

Try to integrate performance tests into your pipeline

Don't let performance testing for something later. Include it as part of your build process, so that you can catch performance issues before they happen. In fact, you can even fail your builds if a commit causes a performance regression and prevent it from going any further. If performance is important for your project, consider adding performance as part of your continuous integration. It can let you prevent performance regressions before they get shipped.

The sooner you are aware of regressions, the easier they are to fix. In large code bases, small regressions can build up over time unless they're aggressively kept in check. Tests can keep them out of your system. Yes, it's difficult to run these all the time and it can slow down the pipeline a little, but honestly what takes longer, the extra few minutes to run the pipeline or the many hours of debugging to find your performance issue?

I will discuss performance testing in more detail later in the book, but I did want to make it clear early on already that the testing of your systems shouldn't be left till later in the cycle and should form part of your code testing objectives.

Challenges to Code Optimization

Before I talk about some coding patterns or designs that might help with this efficiency, I want to look at some common challenges, so that you can also consider all the aspects of whether you SHOULD optimize the code or not. Often, given the challenges below, tweaking your code further is just not worth the effort and so understanding all the different elements to look at, should help you and your team to make the right choice.

Understanding the level of gain

You need to know not only how fast (or memory-intensive, etc.) the system is, but also how much marginal gain you will get from improvements. Do you save your company money? Do you save your users time? If it is a script that runs once a week that nobody is dependent on? Even savings of an entire minute (basically forever in computer time) might not be worth adding complexity. But if it's a function run a million times per second across a fleet of thousands of servers, savings of microseconds could save a lot of money.

If you understand what your performance goals are before beginning your work, you can make the right call on performance/complexity trade-offs later on. If you are being honest with yourself, you will often see that you should scrap marginal gains and focus on major wins.

Finding the balance

Fast code is not necessarily the most maintainable or "easiest to read" way of coding (as discussed in the earlier chapter on Maintainable Code). While it makes a lot of sense to always opt for the most optimal route, in a bigger organization you need to fit into the bigger picture and find the balance between speed and simplicity. A lot of this decision will rest on how important speed is to the piece of code you are working on though or how often you expect the code to be maintained.

Keeping the rest of the system in mind

Often your code doesn't sit in isolation and needs to interact with other parts of the system. For back-end API code for instance it can often be easy to tweak things for performance, but you also need to remember that if there is integration with a UI element or database, that we aren't just testing our code in isolation, but also in conjunction with how it's been designed.

It sounds obvious, but code optimized for the user experience is not necessarily always the fastest solution for throughput- and the overall aim and objective of what you are trying to achieve needs to be considered.

Third-Party Integration

For many developers and companies' systems do not sit in isolation and need to interact with a solution that belongs to a third party where you cannot optimize its code.

In situations like this, you need to factor in the performance of your third-party system and often what is required for it to run optimally rather than your solutions or preferred methods. This, in particular, becomes tricky in dealing with data or memory management where it might not fit into the way you would like it to work, but you will need to make a change to ensure it can operate optimally in the future. The ideal scenario is to always design your own solutions, but in big connected systems, that is just not possible and so you need to make do with some level of third-party interaction.

Dealing with the data

More often than not, I've found the biggest performance issues can come from the way we handle data. It's not that our code or even SQL is not optimized, but simple that just processing the needed data given the current infrastructure takes too long. There could be many other solutions to look at like changing your databases, archiving your data, reducing the required data in a database, optimizing DB structure, or even introducing parallelization where you can distribute your data and run query across multiple servers, thereby increasing throughput.

Ultimately there are a lot of ways to optimize databases, and these should be explored in detail. I do discuss some solutions later in this chapter, but the nature of data engineering is far too complex and detailed for the intentions of this book, so would rather encourage you to do your own research in this regard or speak to your relevant data experts.

Understanding how your compiler works
In learning how to optimize code, you also need to learn to understand the language and its compiler. Sometimes, your performance constraints could be a result of your compiler and you need to code in a way that will allow your compiler to optimize most efficiently.

The way Java works is different from Python or C++ and so understanding some of the small nuances of the underlying compiler helps in identifying ways that your code can work quicker. Some compilers control some of these optimizations for you, some leave these completely up to the developers. So, be aware of these differences because it will determine exactly how much of the optimization you can control or at times, even if you are using the right programming language for the efficiency you require. If you want absolute performance, go as low as possible and program in machine or assembler code – though this would be overkill for many products.

Throwing better hardware at the problem

While this is very tempting to resolve issues quickly. Throwing more hardware at a problem is not a permanent solution for inefficient code. Yes, it might alleviate current constraints or mask them for a short while, but poorly performing code will likely continue to affect you as you scale or tax your system more, only exasperating the problem for later. So, if you need to quickly resolve a production issue, sure throw more hardware at it for now – but get the code optimized before you forget about it.

Optimizing Your Code

Once you've gone through all these different challenges and come to the conclusion that your code or solution still needs to be optimized, then it is time to start approaching how you can go about designing better code that runs optimally.

Whether writing code from scratch or trying to improve existing code, optimizing your code is a tricky prospect, but that doesn't mean that there aren't a few tricks to be aware of that could help you make some performance gains in your code. While these examples don't apply equally to every solution, language, or compiler, its important concepts nonetheless that could help to improve the performance of your code.

Not everything is applicable to every situation or compiler and the intent here is just to give you things to look out for and hopefully provide ideas for how to make your code more optimized. The most important thing is to find the most appropriate solution that meets what you require. Some other important pointers to consider are:

- You could optimize your code for performance using all possible techniques, but this might generate a bigger file with a bigger memory footprint.

- You might have two different optimization goals that might sometimes conflict with each other. For example, optimizing the code for performance might conflict with optimizing the code for less memory footprint and size. You might have to find a balance.

- Performance optimization is a never-ending process. Your code might never be fully optimized. There is always more room for improvement to make your code run faster.

- Sometimes you can use certain programming tricks to make code run faster at the expense of not following best practices such as coding standards, etc. Try to avoid implementing cheap tricks to make your code run faster.

How do you calculate true optimization?

Code optimization is not simply getting code to execute quicker in a testing cycle. There are a lot of different factors that affect how code performs and in understanding how to calculate some aspects of code optimization, it can help you to identify areas in your code that may be inversely affecting its performance.

It's difficult to measure the speed of your code because each line of code doesn't translate into an actual CPU operation, where decision trees, loops, and memory management all play a bigger part of ensuring your code is optimal. There are

Quality by Design

also external factors like hardware (cache, CPU, or GPU types), operating systems, or - for the web - different rendering engines, which also play a part in how your code will perform.

Keeping all this in mind though, these are some big things to consider in the practice of writing optimized code:

Using the appropriate algorithm
Speed is not simply about the easiest way of solving a problem or often even the shortest but needs to consider CPU processing. Ideally, what you want to do when optimizing any algorithm is figure out which decision tree or branch logic will require the least number of options to work through – or alternatively least CPU time.

Consider the following scenario: We have an interval for x [-100...100] and an interval for y [-100...100]. Now in these two intervals, we are looking for a maximum of the function (x*x + y*y)/ (y*y + b).

This is a function of two variables: x and y. There is one more constant that could be different, and a user will enter it. This constant b is always greater than 0 and lesser than 1000.

In this example, I don't want to make use of any prebuilt math functions, though I would be interested to see how optimized some of the prebuilt functions we rely on in our languages are.

Example code (in C++):
#include <iostream>
#define LEFT_MARGIN_FOR_X -100.0

```
#define RIGHT_MARGIN_FOR_X 100.0
#define LEFT_MARGIN_FOR_Y -100.0
#define RIGHT_MARGIN_FOR_Y 100.0

using namespace std;
int
main(void)

{
//Get the constant value
cout<<"Enter the constant value b>0"<<endl;
cout<<"b->"; double dB; cin>>dB;
if(dB<=0) return EXIT_FAILURE;
if(dB>1000) return EXIT_FAILURE;

//This is the potential maximum value of the function
//and all other values could be bigger or smaller
Double dMaximumValue =
(LEFT_MARGIN_FOR_X*LEFT_MARGIN_FOR_X+LEFT_MARGI
N_FOR_Y*LEFT_MARGIN_FOR_Y)/
(LEFT_MARGIN_FOR_Y*LEFT_MARGIN_FOR_Y+dB);

double dMaximumX = LEFT_MARGIN_FOR_X;
double dMaximumY = LEFT_MARGIN_FOR_Y;
for(double dX=LEFT_MARGIN_FOR_X;
dX<=RIGHT_MARGIN_FOR_X; dX+=1.0)
 for(double dY=LEFT_MARGIN_FOR_Y;
dY<=RIGHT_MARGIN_FOR_Y; dY+=1.0)

  if( dMaximumValue<((dX*dX+dY*dY)/(dY*dY+dB)))
  {
   dMaximumValue=((dX*dX+dY*dY)/(dY*dY+dB));
   dMaximumX=dX;
```

```
    dMaximumY=dY;
  }
```

```
cout<<"Maximum    value    of    the    function    is="<<
dMaximumValue<<endl;
cout<<endl<<endl;
```

```
cout<<"Value for x="<<dMaximumX<<endl
  <<"Value for y="<<dMaximumY<<endl;
        return EXIT_SUCCESS;
}
```

Now, if we analyze the code more carefully, we notice that the part for dX*dX is calculated more times than it should, in this case, it is calculated 200 times, and this is a waste of CPU time.

There are several solutions to solve this, but perhaps the most basic would be to create one variable (dX_Squer = dX*dX) and calculate after the first for repetition. This could then be used in all calculations afterward. You just need to add one more bracket.

There are a few more optimizations that can be made in the above code, but I'll leave these for you to figure out.

Optimize Your Code for Memory
Now we will look at how you could optimize your code from point of memory consumption.

Let us take a simple example. Let us try to swap two values in the memory, which is done in many sorting algorithms.

Some people like to think of this as two people sitting on two chairs and adding one more chair as a temporary holder for one of them during the swap.

```
int nFirstOne =1, nSecondOne=2;
int nTemp = nFirstOne;
nFirstOne = nSecondOne;
nSecondOne = nTemp;
```

This is nice but actually saves extra variables in memory. This could be done without nTemp like this:

```
int nFirsOne = 3, nSecondOne = 7;
nFirstOne += nSecondOne;
nSecondOne = nFirstOne ? nSecondOne;
nFirstOne -= nSecondOne;
```

In some cases, you could have large objects in memory that need to swap their places. So, what could you do? Instead of coping with many memory locations, you could use their addresses and instead of replacing the memory locations you could just change their address.

Problems with Functions
While we utilize functions because it makes our code more modular, maintainable, and scalable, if we are not careful, functions can create some performance bottlenecks.

For example, functions don't work well in loops:
```
for(int i=1; i<=10; ++i)
   DoSomething(i);
```

It certainly makes your coding shorter, but repeatedly calling a function to do a similar thing 10 times is an unnecessary expenditure on your memory. To implement this better, you should rather implement the repetition directly in your function. This would require less processing.

The next thing to consider is inline functions. And there are other things we can look at which do it better. For instance, if they are small, you can make use of macros. This way you benefit from a point of speed, from point of better organization, and as well as reusability.

When passing a big object to a function, you could use pointers or references. Prefer to use references because they would create the code that is way easier to read.

If you are not worried about changing the value that is passed to the function, use references. If you use an object that is constant, it could be useful to use const, which will save some time.

Optimizing Loops
While recursion is extremely helpful in certain specific scenarios, in general, it will generate a slow-performing code. If possible, try to avoid recursion, when you don't need to use it to solve your problem.

Before:
for(i=0;i<100;i++) {
    map[i].visited = 0;
  }

After:
i=99;

```
do {
  map[i].visited = 0;
  i--;
} while(i>=0);
```

Loops serve a purpose, but you want to reduce your reliance on them and rather only attempt it if it is needed a few times with several operations needed within it.

Otherwise, if you need to iteratively sort through something, use another type of sorting algorithm to reduce your processing time.

Data Structure Optimization
Much like most things, data has a big impact on our code performance, and the way we structure the data we need to use in our code will play a big part in enhancing the speed of our code.

If you keep your data in the list, you could very easily create a program that will outperform one with the array we have mentioned. Sometimes, if you save your data in some form of tree you could create a program that will perform faster than the one without adequate data structure.

Be careful when using data structures though. Sometimes a problem could be solved without keeping all elements of an array or using any data structure at all.

Binary Search or Sequential Search
One of the common tasks we need to do when we program is to search for some value in some data structure. Yes, it is the basis for hash tables, multi-level hash tables, etc.

If you are trying to find one number in an array of numbers, you could have two strategies.

The first strategy is very simple. You have the array and value you are looking for. From the beginning of the array, you start to look for the value and if you find it you stop the search, and if you don't find the value you will be at the end of the array. There are many improvements to this strategy.

The second strategy requires the array to be sorted. If an array is not sorted, you will not get the results that you wish for. If the array is sorted, you split it into two halves. In the first half, the elements of an array are smaller than the middle one in another half the elements are bigger than the middle one. If you get yourself in a situation where two markers are not situated the way that they should be, you know that you do not have the value you have been looking for.

If you sort elements of an array, you will lose some time, but if you invest in that you could benefit from a faster binary search.

This is one of several situations where you would need to understand the problem well and act according to the best possible situation based on your specific scenario.

Optimizing Arrays
The array is one of the most basic data structures that occupy some space in memory for its elements.

To understand how these optimizations work, you should be

aware of the structure of the array. The name of an array is a constant pointer that points at the first element of an array. This means that you could use pointers and pointer arithmetic.

for(int i=0; i<n; i++) nArray[i]=nSomeValue;

Instead of the above code, the following is better:
for(int* ptrInt = nArray; ptrInt< nArray+n; ptrInt++)
*ptrInt=nSomeValue;

The reason for this is in the operations with pointers. In the above example, we have a pointer to the int data type that takes the address from the name of the array. In this case, it is nArray, and we increase that address for one element, and the pointer is moved toward the end of the array for the size of the int data type.

If you have used double, your compiler would know how far it should move the address.

It is harder to read code this way, but it will increase the speed of your program. In other words, when you don't use a better algorithm, but your program still runs faster, the increased speed might be due to better syntax that will generate faster code.

If you use a matrix, and you have the chance to approach the elements of the matrix row by row or in some other manner you should always pick to go row after the row in your matrix. The matrix is an array of arrays it will be stored in memory row after the row, so the most natural way to approach the array members is to go row by row.

Avoid initialization of large portions of memory with some element. If you could not avoid this type of situation, consider memset or similar commands.

Using Operators
Most basic operations like +=, -=, and *=, when applied to basic data types could slow down the program as well. To be sure you will need to know how it gets transformed into assembler code on your computer.

One interesting idea is to replace postfix increment and decrement with their prefix versions.
Sometimes you could try to use operators >> or << instead of multiplication or division, but be very careful, you could end up with a bad mistake this way, and then to fix it you could add some range estimations and that will be way slower than the original code you have started with.

Bit operators and tricks that go with them could increase the speed of a program, but you should be very careful because you could end up with machine-dependent code and that is something to avoid.

Using tables versus recalculating
Tables are often easier to work with and the simplest solution to code, but don't scale well. Remember that in recalculating, you have the potential of using parallelism, and incremental calculation with the right formulations. Tables that are too large will not fit in your cache and hence may be very slow to access and cannot be optimized further. Much like the data structures described earlier in the chapter – tables should be used with caution.

Using smaller data types is faster than larger ones
The original reason int was put into coding languages was so that the fastest data type on each platform remained abstracted away from the programmer himself. On modern 32 and 64-bit platforms, small data types like chars and shorts actually incur extra overhead when converting to and from the default machine word-sized data type.

On the other hand, one must be wary of cache usage. Using packed data (and in this vein, small structure fields) for large data objects may pay larger dividends in global cache coherence, than local algorithmic optimization issues.

Use powers of two for multidimensional arrays

Before:
char playfield[80][25];

After:
char playfield[80][32];

The advantage of using powers of two for all but the leftmost array size is when accessing the array. Ordinarily, the compiled code would have to compute a multiply to get the address of an indexed element from a multidimensional array, but most compilers will replace a constant multiply with a shift if it can. Shifts are ordinarily much faster than multiplies.

Data type considerations

Often to conserve space you will be tempted to mix integer data types; chars for small counters, shorts for slightly larger counters, and only use longs or ints when you really must. While this may seem to make sense from a space utilization point of view, most CPUs end up wasting precious cycles converting from one data type to another, especially when preserving signs.

Before:
char x;
  int y;
    y = x;

After:
 int x, y;
   y = x;

Conclusion

The above list is in no way exhaustive, nor complete, but hopefully will help you to think about optimization in your code a little more. Similarly, continue to play around with your different compilers and coding languages to determine which ones may work best for you and find that perfect balance between form and function. Writing fast code is important but can slow down your productivity and you want to make sure it's worth your while to do.

However, if you practice these tricks and make them a habit, writing optimized code can become more natural to you.

Diving Deeper into Performance Testing

Having now discussed how to design software that caters for performance, I want to also dive deeper into the importance of performance testing and specifically how to approach it and what to look for and measure in order to get the best value out of your performance testing approach to better identify areas for performance improvement.

So, in this chapter, I hope to provide you with a bit more insight on what to specifically test for to help ensure your software meets its performance expectation and also enable you to identify the right performance bottlenecks so that you can address those constraints/bottlenecks a little further.

One of the key parts of performance testing is the tools involved. There are many to choose from, but they all typically work and test around the same principles. As a result, I won't go into any analyses over the tools to choose, but rather just provide a good foundation of what you need to look for to test system performance adequately.

Firstly, we'll look at the different types of Performance Testing. While we commonly use the phrase "performance testing" to focus on the performance of our software, it is actually the culmination of a variety of testing techniques, which all look at different angles of software performance and reliability and help to identify different performance bottlenecks.

Load Testing

Checks the application's ability to perform under anticipated user loads. The objective is to identify performance bottlenecks before the software application goes live.

Stress Testing

Involves testing an application under extreme workloads to see how it handles high traffic or data processing. The objective is to identify the breaking point of an application.

Endurance Testing

This type of testing is done to make sure the software can handle the expected load over a long period of time.

Spike testing

Tests the software's reaction to sudden large spikes in the load generated by users.

Volume Testing

Under Volume Testing large no. of. Data is populated in a database and the overall software system's behavior is monitored. The objective is to check the software application's performance under varying database volumes.

Scalability Testing

The objective of scalability testing is to determine the software application's effectiveness in "scaling up" to support an increase in user load. It helps plan capacity addition to your software system.

Diving Deeper into Performance Testing

Common Performance Problems

Most performance problems revolve around speed, response time, load time, and poor scalability. Speed is often one of the most important attributes of an application. A slow-running application will lose potential users. Performance testing is done to make sure an app runs fast enough to keep a user's attention and interest. Look at the following list of common performance problems and notice how speed is a common factor in many of them:

Long Load time - Load time is normally the initial time it takes an application to start. This should generally be kept to a minimum. While some applications are impossible to make load in under a minute, Load time should be kept under a few seconds if possible.

Poor response time - Response time is the time it takes from when a user inputs data into the application until the application outputs a response to that input. Generally, this should be very quick. Again, if a user has to wait too long, they lose interest.

Poor scalability - A software product suffers from poor scalability when it cannot handle the expected number of users or when it does not accommodate a wide enough range of users. Load Testing should be done to be certain the application can handle the anticipated number of users.

Bottlenecking - Bottlenecks are obstructions in a system that degrade overall system performance. Bottlenecking is when either coding errors or hardware issues cause a decrease in throughput under certain loads. Bottlenecking is often caused by one faulty section of code. The key to fixing a bottlenecking issue is to find the section of code that is causing the slow down and try to fix it there. Bottlenecking is generally fixed by either fixing poor running processes or adding additional Hardware.

Some common performance bottlenecks are:

- CPU utilization
- Memory utilization
- Network utilization
- Operating System limitations
- Disk usage

Performance Testing Process

The methodology adopted for performance testing can vary widely but the objective for performance tests remains the same. It can help demonstrate that your software system meets certain pre-defined performance criteria. Or it can help compare the performance of two software systems. It can also help identify parts of your software system which degrade its performance.

Below is a generic process on how to perform performance testing:

Identify your testing environment

Know your physical test environment, production environment, and what testing tools are available. Understand details of the hardware, software, and network configurations used during testing before you begin the testing process. It will help testers create more efficient tests. It will also help identify possible challenges that testers may encounter during the performance testing procedures.

Identify the performance acceptance criteria

This includes goals and constraints for throughput, response times, and resource allocation. It is also necessary to identify project success criteria outside of these goals and constraints. Testers should be empowered to set performance criteria and goals because often the project specifications will not include a wide enough variety of performance benchmarks. Sometimes there may be none at all. When possible, finding a similar application to compare to is an effective way to set performance goals.

Plan & design performance tests

Determine how usage is likely to vary amongst end-users and identify key scenarios to test for all possible use cases. It is necessary to simulate a variety of end-users, plan performance test data and outline what metrics will be gathered.

Configuring the test environment

Prepare the testing environment before execution. It's important that the test environment is set up in a way that is as representative of production as possible. This doesn't mean it needs to be as fast as production but needs to be configured and set up on the server, in the same way, to give predictable and comparable performance even if not exact. As long as your benchmarks are consistent with the test environment, they should be consistent in production.

Implement test design

Create the performance tests according to your test design. What this means is that your different tests should cater to actual possible use-cases and try and be as relevant to customer experience as possible. While it is great to just hit every API and UI object with random data to see if they still function, the truth is that user journeys will often carry with them their own specific data constraints and thereby it's important that your tests cater for the.

Run the tests

Execute and monitor the tests. To execute the tests, you will want your tool to be on a machine separate from your test environment and preferably with a fair amount of power. The reason for this is you do not want a slow machine hampering your results, plus if the tool is sitting on the same server, the additional strain the tool is placing on the processor will skew your analysis.

The real trick with any form of performance testing lies not in the scripting and execution of them, but rather in the monitoring. It's the information that is gained from the different monitors you have created (explained below) that provides you with the most information and helps to identify what is really going on with your system.

Analyze, Tune and Retest

Consolidate, analyze, and share test results. Then fine-tune and test again to see if there is an improvement or decrease in performance. Since improvements generally grow smaller with each retest, stop when bottlenecking is caused by the CPU. Then you may have the consider option of increasing CPU power. This phase of testing can be particularly problematic if you have left performance testing too late, as there could be several poorly optimized components in your system, all of which will need to be rectified individually to verify if they do change performance effectively.

Performance Testing Metrics: Parameters Monitored

The basic parameters monitored during performance testing include:

- Processor Usage - an amount of time the processor spends executing non-idle threads.
- Memory use - the amount of physical memory available to processes on a computer.
- Disk time - the amount of time the disk is busy executing a read or write request.
- Bandwidth - shows the bits per second used by a network interface.
- Private bytes - number of bytes a process has allocated that can't be shared amongst other processes. These are used to measure memory leaks and usage.
- Committed memory - the amount of virtual memory used.
- Memory pages/second - number of pages written to or read from the disk in order to resolve hard page faults. Hard page faults are when code not from the current working set is called up from elsewhere and retrieved from a disk.

- Page faults/second - the overall rate in which fault pages are processed by the processor. This again occurs when a process requires code from outside its working set.
- CPU interrupts per second - is the average number of hardware interrupts a processor is receiving and processing each second.
- Disk queue length - is the average number of read and write requests queued for the selected disk during a sample interval.
- Network output queue length - length of the output packet queue in packets. Anything more than two means a delay and bottlenecking needs to be stopped.
- Network bytes total per second - rate which bytes are sent and received on the interface including framing characters.
- Response time - the time from when a user enters a request until the first character of the response is received.
- Throughput - rate a computer or network receives requests per second.
- Amount of connection pooling - the number of user requests that are met by pooled connections. The more requests met by connections in the pool, the better the performance will be.
- Maximum active sessions - the maximum number of sessions that can be active at once.
- Hit ratios - This has to do with the number of SQL statements that are handled by cached data

instead of expensive I/O operations. This is a good place to start for solving bottlenecking issues.

- Hits per second - the no. of hits on a web server during each second of a load test.
- Rollback segment - the amount of data that can rollback at any point in time.
- Database locks - locking of tables and databases need to be monitored and carefully tuned.
- Top waits - are monitored to determine what wait times can be cut down when dealing with how fast data is retrieved from memory
- Thread counts - An application's health can be measured by the no. of threads that are running and currently active.
- Garbage collection - It has to do with returning unused memory back to the system. Garbage collection needs to be monitored for efficiency.

Example Performance Test Cases

So, we've looked quite extensively at the different aspects of performance testing and what would likely cause performance issues in any given system, but there is still the matter of actually scripting your test cases. As I mentioned earlier, your test cases need to be relevant (though not exclusively) to your typical user journey, but then there is still the matter of knowing how to apply these scripts to get the results you need.

And while to do this effectively on any given system takes a significant amount of understanding of the system itself and how it works, the below test ideas should help to get you started in scripting scenarios that should unearth likely performance issues in your system:

- Verify response time is not more than 4 secs when 1000 users access the website simultaneously.
- Verify the response time of the Application Under Load is within an acceptable range when the network connectivity is slow
- Check the maximum number of users that the application can handle before it crashes.
- Check database execution time when 500 records are read/written simultaneously.
- Check CPU and memory usage of the application and the database server under peak load conditions
- Verify the response time of the application under low, normal, moderate, and heavy load conditions.

During the actual performance test execution, vague terms like acceptable range, heavy load, etc. are replaced by concrete numbers, as you will want to measure against the specific goal that would meet the needs of your software. These numbers should typically form part of the business requirements, and the technical landscape of the application and be discussed during the planning of a particular part of the system.

When to Performance Test

A lot of people leave their performance testing for quite late in the development cycle, once the software is complete and stable. While there is merit to this to get a sense of how everything works together, performance testing should take place at all stages. Leaving it too late to identify and rectify performance issues is expensive and likely to add serious delays to the delivery of every system. In this age of predictability, it's not something you can afford.

Any piece of code or database change should essentially be performance tested as soon as possible to help identify any immediate bottlenecks and optimization deficiencies. I have written previously about how to do this easily at a code level. However, it's not just testing any piece of code, it's testing each API and DB process, and then testing whenever a change is introduced into a system – even hardware changes.

The bottom line is you shouldn't compromise performance in any way and as such, you want to test often and everywhere.

Performance is just as vital to the success of any system/application as its functional quality and so you need to place just as much emphasis on testing and monitoring this throughout your development cycle as you would the rest of your functional testing.

Diving deeper into UI testing

We introduced testing earlier in the book and placed a specific emphasis on building testing frameworks and unit testing. I now want to spend time exploring other forms of testing. Even if we have clear requirements that race well to our code and 100% code coverage at a unit test layer, it doesn't mean that the integrated components of the software will still work well together. Which is why it is so important to test aspects of your UI, API, and Databases separately.

The focus of UI testing is to ensure that all the completed UI elements load and work correctly on the page. Even if most of the deep technical testing should happen at a Unit or API level, UI testing will always remain crucial because it is the form of testing that best verifies the software from a user's perspective and based on what and how the user will use the software.

UI is more than simply putting a pretty face to your software but is a vital part of a customer experience of your software system, and a poor-quality UI system will give the impression of a poor-quality system, even if the backend code is working as expected.

The reason why I am choosing to focus on UI testing as a deep dive first over API or DB testing, which often operate at a lower level, is because it is often the first layer of testing that testers are introduced to, even if this is incorrect. Some of this is historic bias on testing at a front-end level, other reasons could be technical with backend developed by separate teams or third parties. So, even if you never get involved at a lower level of testing, the focus of this chapter is to help ensure that the UI testing is at least done right.

In this deep dive chapter - and with all the other following chapters - I will look at both elements of how to test these areas of your software system and the best practices to automate them separately, because there are different focus areas that apply to each to do them correctly. While we should always develop software and look to test with automation in mind, we need to ensure healthy test analysis is still considered first and then focus on the automation thereof.

While UI testing has traditionally been done after development in a test environment for the testers and focuses more on an end-to-end journey, with certain new stacks it can be easy to test and automate this while the code is still in development too.

Depending on your software architecture, you are likely not going to need to do extensive functional or user journey testing at this phase and you are rather just looking at the visual aspects of how the page renders and ensuring that they display as expected. Sounds easy when described but can be quite complicated to execute correctly.

Firstly, just as any front-end developer can attest to the compacted nature of UI development, so do the same things apply to the testing side of things. There are a multitude of browsers, screen sizes, resolutions, and even devices that all need to be catered for, and to do exhaustive checks on every single screen across each of these items is not only time-consuming, but improbable. Rather your time is best spent on prioritizing where you are likely going to target most of your users and then visually testing from there.

Following the below guidelines should help you to prioritize and plan your UI testing effectively. I will talk about UI testing and UI automation separately, as you need to understand how to test a UI effectively before you can even begin to look at how to automate it:

Tips for Testing the UI

1)   Understand the core functional journey of the UI

While it's difficult to lock down the exact design of a UI, the overall purpose of any new design feature and how it should function needs to be in place and teams shouldn't look to do any development work before this has been finalized otherwise it could lead to waste effort.

As a tester, you would want to know the operational steps of a UI and what test scenarios to look out for as early as possible. Too many companies, for the sake of agility, try and rush this step and rather play around trying to find the right approach at a code level. This is great as a proof of concept, but terrible for the quality of your application so unless you are literally doing a POC, don't follow this approach.

Rather map out the details of how the software is intended to function and start putting together testing criteria upfront to make it easier for the UI developers to build something that matches the testing needs rather than retrofitting testing to the UI.

2)   Standardize design objects

We've already spoken about the importance of testability in writing testable code and the role it plays at a UI level, so I won't go over this again. However, needless to say, it's an important part of the testing process and before we focus on designing our tests, we need to ensure we have clear guidelines in how we will build and standardize our different UI objects to make them more testable.

What this means is that all similar UI components whether they are text boxes, links, or buttons, should all behave in a consistent way, follow a consistent naming convention and be uniquely identifiable by your UI tool based on this naming convention.

As a team, developers and testers should either work together to develop these standards and ensure they are implemented in the code or give the testers the ability to make the changes to the objects themselves to make them more testable.

3)   Know your integration points

While things like APIs and most backend code can be easily segmented into independently operating elements, chances are your UI is going to have to intersect with multiple different backend elements to work effectively. So, it's important to understand all the different APIs, backend systems, and databases you will be interacting with and understand how those work.

UI testing is a lot more tightly connecting than you might realize from an integration perspective and while you don't go into detail on parts of the code, you will touch many parts and so it requires a broader understanding of the system. Knowing these details ensures that you as a team design your elements to correctly interact with each unique system while also being aware of that system's constraints and then designing and testing with these in mind.

4) Understand what the UI does and doesn't validate

Knowing exactly where certain validation steps happen, either a UI, BFF, or API layer will help you as a tester to know the amount of focus you should place on testing it. While you want to ensure each element on a page is usable, if the core logic sits elsewhere, rather test it at the level and let your UI testing only focus on what is necessary.

UI testing is not the place where you want to apply your different boundary value analysis or other test permutations, this is best reserved for testing closer to the code, and preferably in your unit tests, as we discussed in the previous chapter.

5) Practice efficient test case design

Because UI testing is more time-consuming, you want to try and test as much functionality as efficiently as possible. Often you can validate 80% of your codebase with only 10-20% of test coverage and so if you map out your coverage correctly, you can greatly reduce your testing effort. You should already know your core customer journeys at this point in time and so have those identified, along with what backend systems are touched where. What you then need to do is map out how you can run through all the core use cases along with all your integration points to ensure you have everything covered.

There are many techniques like Combinatorial Test Design that help with this sort of thing, but they are focused on when you have a high number of combinations, whereas if you have done your design and analysis correctly, this should preferably be existing lower down and not at a UI level, so not of much use here.

6) Attention to detail is important

Once you have an idea of how and what to test functionally, you need to lay out how you are going to ensure that everything is visually displaying as it should. This is where attention to detail is important because even though you might not think about the slight misalignment of your screen on one particular browser, it's what the customer ends up complaining about the most even if the rest of the site functionality works. While no doubt the priority is to ensure everything functionally works first, a lot of this can often be tested at lower levels leaving your UI to be around the rendering of everything and having strong attention to detail is important here.

7) Prioritize your testing

Whereas UI and API tests are a lot faster to test, UI tests take a lot longer as they generally work with a fully rendered screen, thereby meaning that it is important to know which user journeys you would want to pursue as a primary objective and which UI elements are less important. Also, unless your UI is handling all the validation, you only need to focus on mostly happy day scenarios here and can leave other negative testing scenarios for lower levels.

Prioritization is especially important when it comes to deciding which resolutions, browsers, and platforms to support because testing how everything shows itself visually is not feasible. Having a clear idea of which platforms and areas to target allows you to work towards a feasible plan where you can test effectively and not exhaustively

8) Remember security

More than anything, the UI is where security is most vulnerable as it is what customers are exposed to. While every part of a system should be designed and tested with security in mind, your UI is one place where you don't want to take any chances, and a thoroughly secure UI is the best gatekeeper that any system can have from further security vulnerabilities.

We have already discussed security testing earlier, so go back through that chapter to see which parts will apply to your UI and how you can best implement this testing in your projects.

9) Don't focus your performance and load here

The UI too is where many people end up focusing their performance testing. Part of this is because the majority of tools cater towards UI scripting, but the other aspect of it is because you want to try and replicate your user journey and see how the system performance in that regards. There is some truth to that last part, but if you are relying on your performance testing here, it's often too late. Most bottlenecks in performance typically occur at an API or database level and this is where coding can often best be optimized. So, while you do want to run tests at this level, do only a few basic journeys and leave most of the performance and load tests where they are most likely to surface issues earlier.

UI testing is time-consuming and not always fun but remains one of the most practiced and important parts of many companies testing efforts Learning how to do it properly and focusing on good design and analysis rather than just pure validation though, helps to reduce the testing effort and will especially help when it comes to automation, which I will go into detail about next.

Diving Deeper into UI Automation

The biggest challenge of UI automation though is that it is incredibly flaky in execution as UI testing is not as easily defined and constrained as other lower testing levels, meaning that even though you will have fewer tests in this area, it could often be the most complex aspect of the system to automate effectively. Ultimately you want to prioritize your automation efforts on Unit Tests, with API

Components and integration tests also taking up a large part of the required coverage, but where you do need to still to automate at a UI level, the below guidelines should help to ensure you do this right.

Automate User Behavior and not technical requirements

Where other levels of testing should focus on all the technical details of the application along with business criteria, your UI automation should be focused primarily on the behavior of the software. You aren't trying to test how the software works technically, unit and components test can do that, UI automation should focus on ensuring that the software works the way a user would use it. However, this doesn't just mean that you need to automate these behaviors, but also design your tests around these behaviors – essentially following a form of behavior-driven development.

This doesn't just make tests easier to understand at a business and non-technical level, but also a strict code organization pattern to avoid code duplication. This is done by having separate components called steps or actions that will be the building blocks for your tests so that our actual tests themselves remain relatively simple:

```
@Test

public void someTest() {

  // given

  Something something = getSomething();

= // when
```

something.doSomething();

// then

assertSomething();

}

Try Snapshot Testing

Again, a lot of the testers fail to understand the purpose of their UI tests. While part of UI testing is to ensure the successful integration of your different components through the UI, it is also there to ensure that visually everything renders and displays as expected. The thing is though depending on your architecture, you don't necessarily need to have a site fully operational to see what the UI will look like fully rendered.

Some frameworks can allow you to render the UI components at requested resolutions and screen sizes in a static manner where it can then be compared against a visual snapshot from a previous successful run.

This has pros and cons though. While it certainly speeds up the execution of your automation effort as these tests will run a lot quicker, it doesn't cater to how certain devices or browsers may still render components a little differently. Additionally, it also places a lot of reliance on your screenshots being compared accurately, something which can be easily offset by the slightest rendering error.

I think snapshot testing is a great approach to visual regression given its speed, but probably does not catch everything visually. You will still want to automate other integration tests from a UI perspective, but they should simply verify object operation and not the rendering of your screens.

Use Page Object design patterns and principles

UI testing is a hard and treacherous road full of different potholes. However, the same design patterns that make for good code apply to test automation as well and if you design your automation in a modular and maintainable way, you will alleviate many of the issues that cause frustration with automated tests always needing to be reworked.

The concept of Page Objects is to make UI automation tests consistent, avoid code duplication, improve readability, and organize code for web page interaction. During web test creation you always need to interact with web pages and web elements that are presented on these pages (buttons, input elements, images, etc.).

The Page Objects pattern takes this requirement and applies object-oriented programming principles on top of this, enforcing you to interact with all pages and elements as with objects.

This essentially means that for every object on a page that you need to interact with, a function should exist that contains the different behaviors of the project, so that when you are writing an actual test, you simply reference the object on the page, the action you want to be performed on it and where required, then assert the correct outcome on it.

For example, if you need to click on a button, you don't need to care about how to retrieve this button in the test, as it will already be handled in page objects. You should have the object of the page you are looking for and it should already contain the object of the button you are looking for inside it. All you need is to use a reference to this button object and apply the "click" action on it. You can think about all pages and web elements like this:

For each page and element, you need to interact with, you should create a separate object that will be a reference to this web element in your test. Below is an example of how this will work and aid in writing a better test:

```
WebDriver webDriver = thisDriver;

webDriver.navigate().to("www.anysite.com");

String heading =
webDriver.findElement(By.cssSelector(HEADING_ELEMENT)).getText();

Assert.assertEquals(heading, "Welcome to the Site Header");

Assert.assertEquals(webDriver.getTitle(), "Site Header");

Select objectsFromSelectElement = new
Select(webDriver.findElement(By.cssSelector(OPTION_TO_SELECT)));

Select ObjectsToSelectElement = new
Select(webDriver.findElement(By.id(OPTION_TO_SELECT)));

objectsFromSelectElement.selectByValue("1");

objectsToSelectElement.selectByValue("10");

webDriver.findElement(By.cssSelector(FIND_OBJECTS)).click();

    Assert.assertTrue(webDriver.findElements(By.cssSelector(TOTAL_NO_
OBJECTS)).size() > 0);
```

If we instead apply a Page Object pattern and refactor the same test, we see it become much simpler to navigate and understand

homePage.open();

homePage.waitUntilPageLoaded();

Assert.assertEquals(homePage.getTitle(), "Site Header");

Assert.assertEquals(homePage.getHeadingText(), " Welcome to the Site Header!");

homePage.findObjects("1", "10");

Assert.assertTrue(selectPage.getObjects().size() > 0);

To sum up, the Page Objects brings you these benefits:

- Makes your tests much clearer and easy to read by providing interaction with pages and application page elements
- Organizes code structure
- Helps to avoid duplications (we should never specify the same page locator twice)
- Saves a lot of time on tests maintenance and makes the UI automation pipeline faster => reduces costs

This approach will take a considerably longer amount of time to automate at first but reduces your maintenance effort considerably. While it is faster to just write an automated test case that simply performs a given action on the object within the test a lot quicker, it also means that if you interact with the object multiple times, you will have a duplication of the code. Every time the object's specifications or tests need to change, then you need to update the code in every location as opposed to just one place. Particularly important when you consider the handling of error conditions within your object.

If you want to make this test even cleaner and more maintainable, you can introduce one more level of abstraction - steps or keywords. In different frameworks, you might see different names for these modules, but the principles are the same. Steps (keywords) form modules of actions that you can reuse in any test. Once these steps (keywords) modules are written, all you need is to make a reference to the module in your test and you can use all the functionalities provided by these specific modules. The biggest issue with keywords though is that the abstraction is removed to such a degree that the tests become too easy to write from a technical perspective and a gap develops between people that can understand the test in totality and those simply scripting it. This creates key people dependencies and slows down the overall scripting process as the person writing and running the tests has to wait for someone to modify the keyword or object logic rather than do this themselves.

Avoid timeouts unless there are specific test requirements

Timeouts which essentially consist of sleep() or wait() commands are often inserted into scripts because the automation test often runs at a speed faster than the UI itself can respond at. This forces the test to wait a pre-set amount of time before continuing with its actions.

With the behavior of web applications depending on many factors like network speed, machine capabilities, or the current load on application servers, it is possible for environments to slow down and become unpredictable, which is where sometimes adding a timeout can come in handy to give the system enough time to recover from the unpredictability and ensure more accurate test runs.

The problem with timeouts is it slows down the execution of our test pack considerably. Something which does not seem like much if a test contains only a few second's worth of timeout commands.

However, if you consider that there may be a large number of tests that need to be executed many times a day, that number of wasted time escalates considerably. This doesn't just slow down your automation pipeline but makes it less capable as each time you grow your UI coverage and recall those same object interactions with timeouts, you only exasperate the slowdown in test execution.

Timeouts also mask actual performance faults within an application where you can simply just extend the timeout to keep the script working, rather than force the script to fail when things have waited far too long.

Do not run ALL tests across ALL target browsers and platforms

When it comes to manual testing, we understand that we can't test everything and so we tend to prioritize our testing efforts to where they are best optimized. When it comes to automation though, teams try and build in everything that they hadn't gotten to previously through their automation on all tests.

This too is wasteful and unnecessary. Not only is it unnecessary testing, but it also increases the number of tests that need to be automated and maintained which just makes it increasingly wasteful the more browsers and platforms you try and cater for.

Browser-compatibility automation can instead be applied on a limited test suite, which has tests that interact with all web elements and perform all the main workflows at least once. To provide an example let's assume that we need to verify search functionality for three browsers that we need to support (Firefox, IE, Chrome), as well as different search terms combinations (let's say we have 100 terms).

What would you do in this case? Are you going to run all 100 combinations for each browser? No, that doesn't sound wise... Let's start with browser compatibility. All we need is to ensure that the search input, search button, and search result list elements all work fine for all 3 browsers.

Should we run the search 100 times to verify that? Of course not! Just one time would be more than enough to verify the elements' behavior under the different target browsers.

All the other 99 combinations are required just to verify the relevancy of the search. They are not related to browser compatibility testing itself and therefore can be done by using even one browser or even better, through unit or component tests, which don't require rendering and are therefore even faster to execute. Even if you can't test it at a lower level, 99 tests in 1 browser instead of 3 browsers is clearly the better approach.

Take screenshots for failure investigation

Debugging a visual problem requires a visual aid and to do this, you will want your UI automation to take a snapshot when it identifies visual errors. This will help you save a lot of time when investigating the reasons for a test failure. You can implement a mechanism that will make a browser screenshot in case a test failed.

Most tools should come with a mechanism to do this quite effectively, but if not, the following code can come in handy which you can write as part of a separate include file which each test can all when needed.

What is important is to save your screenshots in a format that doesn't take up too much space (.jpg is often better than .bmp or .png), plus you also need to be aware of how much space these images take up on your repo, so it's important to clean them out on a regular basis to not cause any infrastructure problems. This does require teams to ensure they investigate and make use of these screenshot failures and not let the opportunity to investigate them go to waste.

Keep the pipeline green

This is not specific to UI automation, but given the flakiness often experience with UI automation, I find issues with this concept occur most often here, which is why I have made mention of it in this section on UI automation.

On the one hand, this is one of the simplest principles to understand. but on the other, most engineers ignore this rule. By the "green tests policy" I mean that at times you should expect certain tests to fail for a variety of reasons and you will want to then make sure that despite this, you achieve a 100% rate in your pipeline. After all, if a test fails, it should indicate a problem and you don't want to have multiple tests fail on a regular basis in your pipeline just because you are expecting it.

There are situations when an application already has a list of bugs that are prioritized lower, and the team is not going to fix these issues in the foreseeable future. In this case, most of the engineers just ignore these tests. They leave them inside the run and finish up with many red tests at the end of the test execution. Once the test execution is finished, they just go over the failed tests and verify all the red tests are those that are expected to fail due to these existing bugs, or whether there are some new issues.

This is not a very good way of doing things though. Firstly, each time when execution is finished you have no idea if you have some unexpected issues or not. If the result was red and it is still red, the execution run status tells you nothing.

Second, to understand if you really had some unexpected errors or if all these errors were expected, you need to spend some time doing the investigation. If it were only once that would be fine. But test results validation is a repeated process that you will likely do many times a day. This should not be where an engineer is spending their efforts. You are losing a huge amount of time and effort by conducting the same unnecessary checks again and again.

Instead, if you have failed tests in your run that are expected to fail, the best thing you can do is to move them to a separate run and ignore them in the main test execution. This will save you a lot of time when investigating failed builds.

When you separate all the expected failures from the build, you know that if test execution results in at least one red failed test, then it is a real and new issue. In any other case, they should all be green.

Use data-driven instead of repeated tests

While repeated tests are more predictable and give reliable outcomes, they are not system-specific and will often only work in isolated unit and component tests but not fully functioning integrated tests where you can't rely on mocking and want to instead ensure your test is customer-specific and flows through the entirety of the system.

You want to do this because your customers use data in a way that can often not be predicted and is incredibly difficult to accurately create. Now I am not saying you should use actual customer data for this because that would be illegal in many countries, and you should never have access to this anyway. Rather you should use data that is masked and transformed from production data or alternatively has been extensively created to be as representative as possible.

What this then allows you to do is rather than just rely on the same inputs and expected outputs every time your tests run, you can call from a wide variety of data that doesn't always look the same and therefore can test more different behaviors and permutations in your tests – and hopefully find some unexpected defects along the way. Data-driven tests are not just good for UI, but API tests as well, but I think add the most value here which is why I have made mention of it.

It is important to remind that automation is only a part of your UI testing strategy, and your automation strategy can only be as good as the overall test design allows it to be. Thankfully though given the complications of UI testing, we can reduce a lot of the inherent problems to make your automation tests more focused, better designed and a lot easier to maintain. If you can achieve this and ensure most of your functional testing is done at a modular level, you should be able to easily create an effective automated UI test suite that can add value to your company and team for many years to come.

Diving Deeper into API Testing

Whereas the UI represents the look and feel of a particular application, an API is often where most of the functional processing happens and why testers should spend a lot of their time testing and automating in this department to be able to cover the greatest amount of coverage most efficiently.

APIs serve as the integration points for the majority of software, receiving information, processing or transforming it, and then often either returning it or passing it to another system. This important aspect of the system where lots of logic is handled is therefore critical to get right and test appropriately and unlike UI testing, this is not something where you want to apply a risk-based testing approach and only test what's most critical. At an API level, you want to test as much as possible, meaning that you need to understand the details of how it works all the more important.

Following these below points should help to ensure you approach your API testing correctly. As with the previous chapter, I will look at tips for test analysis before going further into specifics for automation.

Tips for Testing APIs

Understanding the requirements of the API

Often when analysts focus on their business requirements, they look at it from a purely business perspective meaning that the UI often tends to be more well documented with requirements than an API. This is something which is sadly mistaken as APIs are where you want to focus the most on in getting your requirement right.

The good news is though that it is also the part of the software that can be most easily defined. Clear input and output responses make it easier to identify the appropriate test permutations and create the relevant data. And the added benefit is that doing it early doesn't just aid in the testing effort and allow the tester to better write test cases - but with APIs more suited to test-driven development than any other part of a software's architecture - it means the developer can easily build their code to meet the test requirements saving a lot of testing issues further down the line.

To get the most out of identifying the correct test permutation though, you will want to understand the function of the APIs quite well. Before writing tests for an API, you will want to know the following about the API to ensure your requirements have captured all the relevant information:

- What is the purpose of this API?
- What is the workflow of the application? How does it function and what does its architecture look like?
- What are the integrations points of the API? Understand all the upstream and downstream systems it works with and what is required from each
- What are the features and functions of the API?
- What are the expected valid and invalid inputs of the API?
- How should the API behave when invalid messages are received?

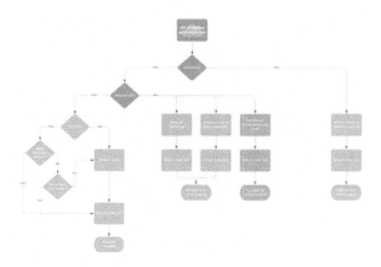

Answering these questions will not only help you know how to test your system but hopefully design it as well and in answering these questions you are likely to identify issues or gaps in your design that may need to be rectified and you would rather want to do there than find it out later during integration testing, so even if this design work takes a lot of extra effort the payoff is worth it.

This information should be clearly documented, particularly the expectations around the different input and output validations and the format of the API messages.

Build a message format

Having the basic requirements and overall flow for your API message sorted out is great, but it is important to at this point build out how your API messages will actually look. You have all the different permutations for testing and development identified in the requirements, but it is helpful to ensure that the overall structure is also well mapped out. This is a time-consuming exercise, but in getting this right, you reduce your development work considerably. It makes it easy for developers to know what to develop towards, makes it easy for testers to write the necessary tests in advance and where dependencies already exist, already start testing again those so you can iron out all your integration points before development is even finished.

Write all the expected input and output messages for your APIs

Now that you have all the relevant information, it's important to document what your API messages and their test criteria will look like. You shouldn't need to wait for an API to be coded to do this but should start it straight away. The input/output of the API tests can vary from pass/fail status to any relevant or invalid data or a call to some other API. The important thing is to be as thorough as possible.

Even if you aren't trying to automate your API, doing this will add some structure to what is needed and form the basis of the developer's design and knowing what their relevant output should look like. The importance of doing this is not just for your current API but also for its other integration points, especially with existing APIs. You can use these to validate that the existing infrastructure and your understanding of these API messages are correct and can prevent any issues before coding is too far along.

Concentrate on Small API Functions

API testing is not a type of testing in which you can directly jump on writing bigger test cases, especially if they cover multiple integration points. So, creating small API test cases or API calls is less painful and likely to give you more immediate results. In small API functions, it then becomes a lot easier to write small API test code and test whether the output is expected or unexpected at each relevant point in an API, rather than waiting for entire integrations to be completed.

Later on, stubbing or including dependencies of the various tiny successful API functions will then be a lot more effective because all of the detailed testing would've already been done, allowing you to focus on positive scenario testing only.

For example, say you want to test the user authentication of an application. If the authenticity of the user is valid, then you want to trigger a password change functionality. While performing API testing here using SOAP/REST, you write two different sets of test cases for two different functions, like user authenticity and password reset. Once you bring the functions together you only need to test one pass through to the second function, saving you a lot of time at an integration level.

Employ Security Testing

Because APIs are integration points to the software, they are key security vulnerability areas. Even though most users many interact via a UI, it is the APIs that receive the messages and where you would want to block any unauthorized or potentially dangerous message. So, once you are done defining all your functional scenarios, it is best to start looking at the security aspects of your API. We've touched on security testing before, but with APIs such an integral point of data flow in an application, I will address some specifics in this chapter too:

To do this, you will want to check your API against the following:

- Various types of SQL, HTML, or code injections. These are often the easiest to test against, as most people should be aware of them, and many security tools will test for these automatically.
- Insecure message connections (your API should not receive a message from certain unsecured APIs)
- Incompatible versions that do not form part of its dependencies – This is an API that is on the list of valid dependencies, but with an out-of-date or incorrect version.
- OS commands – you want to ensure your API detects these and that your OS does not respond as a result when malicious OS commands may be injected into your API.
- Authentication token management – Many sites will make use of an API token that gets sent to ensure a user is validated on a system. You will want to test with a refreshed token or token changes throughout to ensure all entry points can identify the manipulation or duplication of a token ID and its validity.

- I've already discussed security in more detail previous chapter on security testing. As are parts of your application that are highly vulnerable

Measure the performance of the API

APIs might be the functional meat of the system but given that they also serve as the primary flow of information they are central to the overall performance of a system and as such should be performance tested. You don't need to wait for the completion of an integrated system to do this effectively either. You can easily do this once an API is completed and you can performance test with either mocked or unmocked endpoints, pending on the status of the other systems it needs to interact with. Importantly though you want to measure the performance of each individual API in a flow to address the specific performance gaps in that specific API.

To do this, you will want to test how long it takes for an API to execute once it receives its message (start), processes, and passes it on to another (end). All APIs are going to be dealing with different data and systems though, so it's important that you have a certain level of expectation of an API to determine whether the performance tests are meeting expectations. You should also have an expectation for the different load expectations of each API to ensure that you test for these too.

In line with what was mentioned in the chapter on Performance Testing, don't wait for an entire system to be developed before trying to load and performance test your system. These can be done the moment any given API is complete and lightweight performance tests added to your pipeline, to ensure they remain performant throughout its lifecycle.

There is no doubt APIs are an important functional component of any modern software architecture and so you want to invest the effort to ensure you are testing these correctly. One of the biggest benefits of API testing though is that it is significantly easier to automate than a UI and so you want to ensure that once you get your testing approach in order, you make considerable effort to automate these tests, to provide you with good coverage and a high level of confidence in your systems.

Diving Deeper into API Automation

API automation is a lot faster and often easier than UI automation, though that does not mean there is not any complexity in it, and we should focus on it more. Instead, the majority of your end-to-end tests should be focused on at an API level, depending on your architecture and so as such, you want to ensure you understand what goes on here in detail.

Getting your API automation right is also a needed foundation for any attempts at continuous delivery as it enables you to easily tick all the automated integration boxes without as much difficulty as the UI level. So, if you are looking to make full use of your Agile or DevOps process, you will want to definitely incorporate this effectively.

The beauty of automating API tests is that they can often be done without the need for completed code (or at least more easily than frontend tests) and are often simpler to write because there are fewer steps involved. You're simply inputting data (creating a request), potential mocking responses, and then reading outputs (receive a response) and so those are the important things to focus on in the automation process.

Setting up your environment

First is getting your environment ready with the API on it. This may be a shared integrated environment with the API under test in an environment with other APIs that it needs to integrate with. Often though, if you are looking to automate before an API or its dependencies are ready, you will need to set up the environment on your local machine or a personal VM. If you are using some sort of VM/containerization tool, this should be relatively easy to do and replicate across.

Making API calls in your test Framework

The first place to start then with automating your API messages is to ultimately begin to write your different API request messages. Most frameworks have support for making API calls by including an HTTP request library for REST APIs or you can simply just send an XML body to any given location if using SOAP.

When it comes to API automation though I prefer simplicity and the advantage of most frameworks is that there are already a wealth of libraries often built-in that cater to the different API messages that you will need to send, So, I wouldn't recommend reinventing the wheel and simply just taking advantage of the many already excellent libraries out, like superagent for Mocha or Axios and supertest for NodeJS that streamlines the approach and provides all the details you need for a specific message:

```
request

.post('/api/pet')

.send({ name: 'Manny', species: 'cat' }) // sends a JSON post body

.set('X-API-Key', 'foobar')

.set('accept', 'json')

.end((err, res) => {

  // Calling the end function will send the request

});
```

This can handle all different types of GET, PUT, POST, DELETE along with being able to pass headers, cache, and query parameters into the message in an easily parameterized fashion. This saves on needing to build the actual API message in its entirety and makes customizing it for different tests a lot easier

Handling different responses

One of the challenges with API testing is that message responses can come in a variety of formats. Like some may send you a JSON response, others could send an XML, CSV, or other encoded data format based on how they are built. Thankfully, we're in luck again here as most frameworks will support reading of all these. Ideally, you will want to have some idea of how the response message should look so that you can build a response message similar to how you built the request message. The difference here though is that you will also need to make use of an assertion library which will allow you to check for certain parameters in a message, as shown in the below example using chai, which is an assertion library for mocha. (One of the advantages of Jest is the assertion library is built-in, making it just one library to maintain):

response.status.should.equal(200)

foo.should.be.a('string');

foo.should.have.lengthOf(3);

tea.should.have.property('flavors')

.with.lengthOf(3);

If you are using REST, this is made a little easier with its different HTTP Response Codes at least providing some form of standardization that you can search for and immediately assert success based on the response you received.

Informational Response Codes (1xx)

- 100 — Continue, 101 — Switching Protocols, 102 — Processing

Success Response Codes (2xx)

- 200 — OK, 201 — Created, 202 — Accepted, 203 — Non-authoritative Info
- 204 — No Content, 205 — Reset Content 206 — Partial Content, 207 — Multi-status

- 208 — Already Reported, 226 — IM Used, 250 — Low Storage Space

Redirection Response Codes (3xx)

300 — Multiple Choices, 301 — Moved Permanently, 302 — Found, 303 — See Other

304 — Not Modified, 305 — Use Proxy, 307 — Temporary Redirect

308 — Permanent Redirect

Client Error Response Codes (4xx)

- 400 — Bad Request, 401 — Unauthorized, 403 — Forbidden, 404 — Not Found
- 405 — Method Not Allowed, 406 —Not Acceptable, 412 — Precondition Failed
- 415 — Unsupported Media Type

Server Error Response Codes (5xx)

- 500 — Internal Server Error, 501 — Not Implemented, 502 — Bad Gateway
- 503 — Service Unavailable, 504 — Gateway Timeout, 505 — HTTP Version Not Supported
- 506 — Variant Also Negotiates, 507 — Insufficient Storage, 508 — Loop Detected
- 509 — Bandwidth Limited, 510 — Not Extended, 511 — Network Auth Required
- 550 — Permission Denied, 551 — Option Not Supported

- 598 — Network Read Timeout Error, 599 — Network Connect Timeout Error

Handling Test Data

Easily the most difficult part of testing is handling your data. There are multiple approaches from creating your own data, reading data from existing data, another external file (your payload), or possibly even just choosing to randomize the data you send in and out of your API between given attributes.

Which approach you will need to use ultimately depends on the purpose of the test. Because I prefer APIs to be tested largely at a Unit tests level, where it's okay to send through specific messages that return a specific response to determine if your API is handling that message correctly in a case like this, it's easy to set up a JSON or XML file with all the relevant data permutations that can then be inserted into your request message parameters. This body of data for your message is referred to as your payload.

However, while this works for a contained portion of your API, there is a need to test APIS at a more holistic or integrated level and then it makes sense to use data from an actual database to provide more production-specific data or possibly even random data, though I would advise using random data for APIs with very simple message sets and for the purpose of detecting outlier and strange defects.

Many times, while testing though you will require to pass a response from one API as request data to another. You can do so by making use of hooks. Functions like Before, Before each, After, After each, as the name suggests, get executed before/after any or all tests. So, you can use this to arrange for an API test to call and assert on one before it executes another. Given the first point though on where to test, I would recommend keeping this to a minimum.

Configuring your mocks

In these above examples, I have assumed you are testing your API with another API or live endpoint. Often though, you will need to rely on mocks for your automated testing. You might be asking why you would want to mock an API at all when you can test against the real thing.

The problem with this is not only are you often developing an API without all its different dependencies available but that with APIs changing so frequently and integration environments therefore not always proving as reliable as desired, you would still want to rely on some form of mocking to ensure that your API is always operating as expected, regardless of its dependencies.

Yes, there is a need for those non-mocked API tests to check for breaking changes and dependency failures, but the majority of your APIs functionality is internal, and you want to ensure those automated tests remain repeatable and consistent and this is why mocks are so useful. I will go into mocks in more detail later in this chapter.

Running your tests

Given the tool you are using, your test will either be executed from an in-built tool, via a command prompt, or through your

CI tool. These will all look different depending on what you require, so won't go into too much detail on these and would rather encourage you to investigate which solutions work best for you.

What is important is that those environments or environment variables that you configured at the start will need to be called by your automation scripts to prepare your test environments for execution. This is most useful if you are set up for Continuous Integration and require your environments to be pulled together from a different version.

There is ultimately a lot more to API testing than what I go through here, along with a couple of other things to think about like asynchronous messaging in your APIs, integration into CI, and how best to execute and report on these. Not to mention differences in software architectures, programming languages, and frameworks which could alter slight details of the approach. This would probably be enough to cover in a more-specific testing book on its own and is out of scope for what is suitable for this book.

There is a lot to API automation, but despite all these details, API automation is far easier to maintain and easier to implement than UI automation, once you get your head around it. And because it's so much faster to execute and caters to a lower level of testing allows you to do a large number of test permutations in a short space of time.

Mocking APIs

One of the most challenging aspects of API automation though is mocking out API responses. Something which is very important if you want your automation and testing to cover a wide range of coverage without being too dependent on an underlying system or API. Mocking an API call gives you control in these situations and speeds up development down the line.

The biggest challenge of mocking APIs themselves is having the needed information on the underlying systems so that you can sufficiently mock them. In a mock, you want to mimic the behavior of that system and how it responds to your API's own behavior, and to mock this effectively you will need details of exactly how that interaction should look.

This may not always be possible when you start gathering the information to mock, but the side effect of doing this properly is that it forces your teams to better document and understand the different system interactions and in the process of mocking your APIs, you will learn a great deal about its interaction, its dependencies and hopefully have their behavior all documented correctly in the mock itself, so the benefit of doing this far outweighs just its ability to support your automation efforts.

Diving Deeper into Database Testing

No matter your software architecture, the Database is one of the inevitable parts of a Software Application. Data is everything in the information age and even though many people are trying to find ways to alter the way and shape we use data; it will remain a vital part of software development for many years to come and likely only get even more important as we grow and deepen our usage of big data and machine learning.

Whether it is a web, desktop or mobile, client-server, peer-to-peer, enterprise, or individual system the Database is required everywhere at the backend and the same applies across every industry imaginable. And the bigger the complexity of an application increases, the more the need for secure and reliable storage of your data increases. So, no matter your organization or architecture you need to have a database of some sort and because data is the core information by which we make decisions, it is vitally important to ensure that we test our databases effectively

And when it comes to testing, the first place the conversation often turns to is around the tools that we use for testing. There are several different types of database tools on the market like MS-Access, MS SQL Server, SQL Server, Oracle, Oracle Financial, MySQL, PostgreSQL, DB2, Toad, Admirer, etc. Each may differ in cost, robustness, features, and security, but the fundamentals of testing them remain the same. Most of them also come equipped with everything you will need to be able to test your database and the accuracy and consistency of your data, correctly.

However, there is far more to database testing than tooling. And it requires having a bigger understanding of how the software systems utilize their data. Some of which I will try and unpack in this chapter.

Why Test the Database?

The reason why I decided to do a why section here is because so many companies I speak to spend an inordinate amount of simply planning their testing strategies for their APIs or Frontends and put less thought into their database testing. Despite this being a place where so much goes wrong and arguably, has the biggest impact on customers if things go wrong.

#1) Data Mapping

In software systems, data often travels back and forth from the UI (user interface) to the backend DB and vice versa. So, these are some aspects to watch for:

- Checking whether the fields in the UI/frontend forms are mapped consistently with the corresponding fields in the DB table. Typically, this mapping information is defined in the requirements documents.
- Whenever a certain action is performed at the front end of an application, a corresponding CRUD (Create,

278

Retrieve, Update and Delete) action gets invoked at the back end. A tester will have to check if the right action is invoked and whether the invoked action is successful or not.

ACID Properties

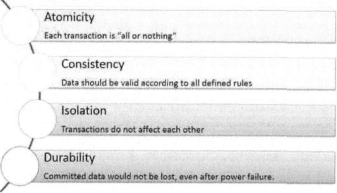

#2) ACID Properties Validation

Atomicity, Consistency, Isolation, and Durability. Every transaction a DB performs must adhere to these four properties. These should be checked in the testing process to ensure they are followed correctly.

Atomicity means that a transaction either fails or passes. This means that even if a single part of the transaction fails- it means that the entire transaction has failed. Usually, this is called the "all-or-nothing" rule.

Consistency: A transaction will always result in a valid state of the DB.

Isolation: If there are multiple transactions and they are executed all at once, the result/state of the DB should be the same as if they were executed one after the other.

Durability: Once a transaction is done and committed, no external factors like power loss or crash should be able to change it

#3) Data Integrity

For any of the CRUD Operations, the updated and most recent values/status of shared data should appear on all the forms and screens. The value should not be updated on one screen and display an older value on another one.

When the application is under execution, the end-user mainly utilizes the 'CRUD' operations facilitated by the DB Tool.

C: Create – When users 'Save' any new transaction, the 'Create' operation is performed.

R: Retrieve – When users 'Search' or 'View' any saved transaction, the 'Retrieve' operation is performed.

U: Update – When users 'Edit' or 'Modify' an existing record, the 'Update' operation of DB is performed.

D: Delete – When a user 'Removes' any record from the system, the 'Delete' operation of DB is performed.

Any database operation performed by the end-user is always one of the above four.

So, DB test cases are needed for checking the data in all the places it appears to see if it is consistently the same.

#4) Business Rule Conformity

More complexity in Databases means more complicated components like relational constraints, triggers, stored procedures, etc. This complexity simply places more importance on testers getting involved and ensuring all these areas are working correctly.

What To Test

So, we know why different database areas need to be tested, but there are perhaps more specifics required to understand some of the actual functional areas that require testing and what you should specifically look at in general with regards to testing specific database operations. In this section, I will get into more specifics of what functional tests are typically expected to be un on your database layer.

#1) Transactions

Transactions are essentially the execution of a SQL statement or command to your database which will alter your data in some form or another, whether it be inserting, deleting, or modifying the data or structure of the database. What is important though is that each of these executions supports the aforementioned ACID properties.

These are the statements commonly used:

BEGIN TRANSACTION TRANSACTION#

END TRANSACTION TRANSACTION#

The Rollback statement ensures that the database remains in a consistent state.

ROLLBACK TRANSACTION#

The rollback statement is something that we often don't place enough emphasis on but is just as important as any other transaction statement, as the ability to reverse any changes is equally as important as executing them.

After these statements are executed, use a Select to make sure the changes have been reflected.

SELECT <items involved in transaction> FROM TABLENAME <tables which involve the transactions>

This is needed to verify that the changes in the transaction have indeed taken place. What is important here is to not do too much of a blanket select statement like 'Select *' as this can take too long to execute and take longer to verify. Your select statement should preferably be just as optimized as your transactional statement.

#2) Database Schemas

A Database Schema is nothing more than a formal definition of how the data is going to be organized inside a DB. You need to ensure this looks and is shaped correctly, even without data. To test it, use the following two steps:

Identify the Requirements based on which the Database operates.

These are specifics within the schema that you can easily test around and ensure consistency through the different tables in a database.

- Primary keys need to be created before any other fields are created.
- Foreign keys should be completely indexed for easy retrieval and search.
- Field names starting or ending with certain characters.
- Fields with a constraint that certain values can or cannot be inserted.

Use one of the following methods according to the relevance:

- SQL Query DESC<table name> to validate the schema.
- Regular expressions for validating the names of the individual fields and their values
- Tools like SchemaCrawler to better visualize the schema of the database.

The good news is that for this there are tools that can help, making the testing approach a lot easier. This means that as long as you have an idea on what to test for, the tools will be able to quickly provide you with the needed information and often even advise you when things are not up to standard.

#3) Triggers

When a certain event takes place on a certain table, a piece of code (a trigger) can be auto-instructed to be executed.

For Example, a new student joined a school. The student is taking 2 classes: math and science. The student is added to the "student table". A Trigger could add the student to the corresponding subject tables once he is added to the student table.

The common method to test is to execute the SQL query embedded in the Trigger independently first and record the result. Follow this up with executing the Trigger as a whole and then compare the results.

These are tested in both the Black-box and White-box testing phases.

White box testing:

Stubs and Drivers are used to insert or update or delete data that would result in the trigger being invoked. The basic idea is to just test the DB alone even before the integration with the front end (UI) is made.

Black box testing:

a) Since the UI and DB, integration is now available; we can Insert/Delete/Update data from the front end in a way that the Trigger gets invoked. Following that, Select statements can be used to retrieve the DB data to see if the Trigger was successful in performing the intended operation.

b) The second way to test this is to directly load the data that would invoke the Trigger and see if it works as intended.

#4) Stored Procedures

Stored Procedures are similar to user-defined functions. They are essentially prepared SQL code that can be saved and reused repeatedly by other functions that call it. You can also pass parameters and other variables into these statements, and they can behave differently based on the inputted data/variable. Think of them like a modularized SQL statement. You can These can be invoked by Call Procedure/Execute Procedure statements and the output is usually in the form of result sets.

#5) Field Constraints

The Default value, Unique value, and Foreign key:

Much like a lot of the elements that we need to test, different fields in a database have specific constraints that determine what they are. And while we shouldn't need to tirelessly test these if we know the structure of the database, we should ensure our systems behave appropriately when inputs that fall outside of these constraints are inputted. If you don't have access to these specific structures and want to test these, then I would recommend the following:

Validate the results with a SQL Query.

Checking the default value for a certain field is quite simple. It is part of business rule validation. You can do it manually or you can use tools For the Foreign Key constraint validation use data loads that directly input data that violate the constraint and see if the application restricts them or not. Along with the back-end data load, perform the front-end UI operations too in a way that will violate the constraints and see if the relevant error is displayed.

Hopefully, it's clear that you need to take your database testing seriously and now have an idea of what to look out for. Now, I will go into further details on what areas specifically testers should focus on and how they can test these areas correctly.

Data is the lifeblood of many a company and so hopefully by placing greater emphasis on ensuring it is tested correctly, it's one area of your software architecture that you can keep working as expected.

Ultimately, there is a lot that is unique to every data source and its structure, so will try and keep things as lightweight as possible, but hopefully, the following guidelines will help to make testing your databases a whole lot easier.

Database Tester Should Focus on the following Testing Activities:

#1) Ensure Data Mapping:

Data Mapping is one of the key aspects of the database and it should be tested rigorously by every software tester.

Make sure that the mapping between different forms or screens of your application and its DB is not only accurate but also per the design documents or code (wherever you get your schematic designs from). Basically, the point of testing here is to validate the mapping between every front-end field with its corresponding backend database fields.

For all CRUD operations, verify that respective tables and records are updated when the user clicks 'Save', 'Update', 'Search' or 'Delete' from the GUI of the application.

What you need to verify:

- To effectively ensure you have achieved the above, you will want to test the following or your different fields.
- Table mapping, column mapping, and Data type mapping.
- Lookup Data Mapping.
- Correct CRUD operation is invoked for every user action at UI.
- CRUD operation is successful.

#2) Ensure ACID Properties of Transactions:

ACID properties of DB Transactions refer to the 'Atomicity', 'Consistency', 'Isolation', and 'Durability'. These four properties should be tested for in each database transaction you test.

Below is a simple example of how this could be done. It's a very basic example of a simple table. No doubt your actual tables will be far more complex, but this guideline should provide a foundation on which you can expand for your different tables:

CREATE TABLE acidtest (A INTEGER, B INTEGER, CHECK (A + B = 100));

The ACID test table will have two columns – A & B. There is an integrity constraint that the sum of values in A and B should always be 100.

Atomicity test will ensure any transaction performed on this table is all or none i.e., no records are updated if any step of the transaction is failed.

A Consistency Test will ensure that whenever the value in column A or B is updated, the sum always remains 100. It won't allow insertion/deletion/update in A or B if the total sum is anything other than 100.

An Isolation Test will ensure that if two transactions are happening at the same time and trying to modify the data of the ACID test table, then these tractions are executing in isolation.

A Durability Test will ensure that once a transaction over this table has been committed, it will remain so, even in the event of power loss, crashes, or errors.

This area demands more rigorous and thorough testing if your application is using the distributed database., as this will only escalate the need for data consistency and conformity across a diverse set of data.

#3) Ensure Data Integrity

Data should look and read the same whether it is displayed in the UI or stored or shared across different databases and systems. Considering that different modules in any system will use the same data in different ways and perform all the CRUD operations on the data, it's important to ensure that not only is data stored correctly throughout, but that the latest state of the data is reflected everywhere.

This is the purpose of data integrity testing and why you need to test it across your entire system in the following areas:

- Check if all the Triggers are in place to update reference table records.
- Check if any incorrect/invalid data exists in the major columns of each table.
- Try to insert wrong data in tables and observe if any failure occurs.
- Check what happens if you try to insert a child before inserting its parent (try to play with Primary and foreign keys).
- Test if any failure occurs if you delete a record that is still referenced by data in any other table.
- Check if replicated servers and databases are in sync.

#4) Ensure the Accuracy of the implemented Business Rules:

Databases have evolved into extremely powerful tools that don't just store data but provide a platform for developers to implement business logic at the DB level. This is useful as it helps ensure referential integrity across the entire system while also reducing impact elsewhere in the system, making applications more scalable and performant if the database features are designed correctly.

Examples of certain features built into dates that you would want to test include Referential Integrity, Relational constraints, Triggers, and stored procedures.

So, using these and many other features offered by DBs, developers implement the business logic at the DB level. The tester must ensure that the implemented business logic is correct and works accurately.

Build Effective Monitoring

Of course, building software is important, but we need to also understand how our system works to be able to better improve it in the future. Even though we are trying to design a reliable and robust system from the beginning, the reality is that how software is used and performs in production is not always how it works in production.

There is also the aspect of software maintenance and being able to respond to underlying issues. Hardware and networks are going to fail, and software attacks are going to occur, no matter how well designed our systems are – and so having an effective monitoring system in place is crucial to being able to do this.

I've already written about how monitoring is effective in understanding performance issues in the performance design and testing chapters. However, I did want to devote an entire chapter to this topic as it is a crucial aspect of software development that doesn't get enough attention.

Designing software along the best quality principles though does already mean that your applications should be well placed to take advantage of monitoring, because their modular design allows processes to be more finely tracked and thereby allow for more accurate analysis, control, and – most importantly – remediation as you scale, adjust, or fix more readily.

It's All About the data

The purpose of monitoring is all about collecting data from the different systems. We do this through running tools that gathered data on the applications, server, or VM performance and pushing that information into a logging tool that can record it.

We then correlate this information into other information we are logging about our own software, that keeps track of all forms of requests and user behavior to these same tools so that we can see how these systems perform against different behaviors. This extra correlation also allows us to have a better understanding of issues when alerts or issues are triggered and better respond and fox them because we can use the data to better understand what is happening on both a hardware and software front.

There are two main types of data here, numbers and letters. If it is numeric data that you are capturing, use a graph. If the data you are capturing is made up of discreet entries, use a log, then graph the log if it makes sense.

Examples of logged data points include successful processes of all kinds:

Data Import/Exports: In many environments, there are data import/export jobs that are critical to applications. That is fine, but you do not want to pollute your email with successful job output, instead put it into a log where it can be properly analyzed.

Granular Job Tracking: When you put job tracking data into a log instead of email, you can start to take advantage of very granular job tracking. Instead of logging success/failure for the whole job, you can start to track individual parts of a job and really get some granularity to your system. This helps track down partial failures like slowdowns, etc.

Load Average, CPU, Memory: Many people make the mistake of thinking these are good fault monitors. They are not, graph them instead. They will help tell you when a problem started after you receive a fault from some other check. Yes, there are limits to these measures which can be used for alerts, but outside of these parameters, we don't really need to keep track of this information on a regular basis.

Route View Checks: Data needs to be routed between different VMs, services, and other locations across a network, both internally and externally. We can use load balancers and Application Delivery Controllers to capture this information, but we need to importantly push this information to a centralized place for full analysis.

Trace Routes: We log trace routes between our data centers to have a historic view of what path things are taking. This can help when troubleshooting flaky VPN connections, but I don't want to know about it unless the VPN gets flaky.

Config File Generation: In many environments, configuration files are built and deployed. Many pieces of this process should be logged. It provides a paper trail for what has been deployed and may be used later if a bug is found in your build process. This will give you a starting point for repairing/rebuilding systems that were deployed during the time the bug was in the wild. It may also help track a start/stop time for when things occurred.

Backup Processes: Parts of the backup process, for example, MySQL dumps, SVN Dumps, and datastore dumbs to different storage locations can be orchestrated and logged from a central script. Your operations team won't need to know this in an email or on a daily basis, but it is a blessing when trying to reverse engineer the system when there is a problem.

Now, you shouldn't forget that there is granularity here. If a particular piece of a process, check, import, etc. fails, you can escalate it to a non-critical or critical action. Sometimes it is even necessary to cause a cascading failure. For example, when collecting data points for a geographically redundant web application, if MySQL replication fails, you may also want to stop the synchronization of a 'docroot' until an operations person can investigate what went wrong.

How to Use the Data

There is a difference between data types though, and some data may be more critical than others and so how we use and show this data will need to differ. While it's nice gathering all this information, you wouldn't want your engineers not being able to respond to issues effectively because they missed alerts because there was too much noise in all the information they were trying to interpret.

We need to correctly understand why we are tracking specific data to better know how to use it in our efforts to improve the quality of our system.

Non-Critical Action

This type of data should be pushed to a dashboard instead of paging. You should expect operations people to look at the dashboard first thing in the morning and periodically throughout the day. These kinds of data points do not need tending in the middle of the night.

You can be a bit more liberal with non-critical alerts, especially if they are fed to a dashboard, but do not get carried away. You do not want to pester your operations people so bad during the day that they can't get project work done

Examples of non-critical actions include failed processes of all kinds

Software Vulnerabilities: These are published on public RSS feeds, but your operations team isn't going to care about this at 02h00 when they are sleeping. They can look at it during business hours. Even if it is a critical vulnerability, no one is going to look at this at 02h00 Many people get this wrong.

SLA in Danger: These kinds of checks can be exceedingly difficult to tune. Four second page load times may be OK at 04h00, but not at 11h00. Sometimes time-based metrics are necessary, but this can require significant scripting or configuration in your monitoring system. I prefer embedding this in the scripting framework because it gives you granular access by check. Often this is difficult to do in something like Nagios.

Captured Command Output: When scripting, use a utility to collect the non-zero output of important commands. If something goes wrong, it should alert you. This provides very granular reporting of failed portions of a script. You can use something called scriptlog to pipe command return values and output to syslog. Then use a Nagios check which captures failed commands and displays a warning in the dashboard. This allows the team to fix problems in the morning and gives a good place to start when fixing scripting problems.

Note, while I mention certain tools here, these are just some that can prove helpful. There are many excellent tools out there and I would encourage you to explore what works best for you and your team.

Critical Action

Do not underestimate how difficult it is to determine these kinds of checks. It is easy to put too many things in this category. If a switch, router, firewall, server, Apache, or the application is in a fault state, someone must be alerted, and the service must be restored but be careful when specifying an SLA for slow service. Make sure they are well defined and manageable. For example, many people will ping network or server gear once a minute and page when it is slow for 2 minutes. This is just impossible to manage, it will page you at 02h00 every day. This is completely useless and when you have a real problem people will end up waiting for a recovery notice and won't even start investigating until the problem seems real

Network Down: It is preferable to monitor the fault state with a true/false check of some kind such as ping. Routers can slow down when updating BGP and do not necessarily indicate an actionable alert unless the slow state persists for long enough.

Server Down: Server down state can be even trickier to determine. Often a server will stop reporting for a while because of heaving processing. If there is enough deviation in your systems, you may even need different checks for different groups of servers.

Service Down: Services can be difficult to check. These checks can become very sophisticated, which makes them impractical for one-minute intervals. In a block, add/delete post can be tested; in a shopping cart, an entire transaction can be tested. These checks can really stretch the boundary between testing and fault monitoring

SLA Not Met: As mentioned above, be very careful when setting these, they can and will drive your operations team insane. Use them sparingly and look for more deterministic ways of finding faults. Also, make sure if the SLA is not met over some number of checks over some number of minutes ore you WILL have false positives

Open Sockets, Pipes, Files: Monitoring open sockets pipes and files can be a very good indication that something is going to go wrong if you don't look into it. If the threshold is high enough it can even indicate impending doom. In production, alerting on these numbers can give you five minutes to respond and fix before a meltdown.

Do not limit your imagination when determining what can be checked but be realistic when determining what it means if a check fails for one, five or ten minutes. When determining an SLA for sophisticated checks, I suggest setting your targets long especially during off-hours. These numbers may sound wild, but I suggest you set the bar low and tune-up. If you desensitize your operations people, your return to service times will be worse than these numbers anyway.

Use Monitoring for Feedback

What would you monitor if you were able to pick and choose your metrics? How many of those metrics would you track and alert on?

Great monitoring systems are driven by purpose. They are designed to provide operational feedback about production systems to people who understand how those systems work. Importantly, these same people have chosen what to monitor about those systems based on that knowledge. The engineers in your organization should understand the metrics you monitor because each metric should have been configured by an engineer to answer a specific question or provide a concrete insight about the operational characteristics of your service.

Monitoring isn't an endeavor unto itself. It is not a backup system or a disaster recovery plan, or any other sort of expensive, labor-intensive burden heaped on Ops to satisfy the checklist requirements of a regulatory body or an arbitrary quarterly goal. It is not a ritual the grown-ups tell us to follow — like always keeping one's hands and arms inside the vehicle — to stave off some nameless danger that no one can quite articulate.

Monitoring is an engineering process. It exists to provide feedback from the things we build, maintain, and care about. It is your best means of understanding the operational characteristics of the systems you depend on. It is the depth gauge in your barrel of money, and the pressure meter on your propane tank. Through monitoring, we gain visibility into places we cannot go. We use it to quantify our success as well as to prevent explosions from happening.

Building quality processes

I am under no allusion that a good design is enough to prevent quality issues in software. At its core, software development remains very much a human operation that involves many different people in different roles working together towards a common goal of producing the desired software product. And this means that outside of just pure architectural design principles, we need to also consider building the right processes.

I know many software practitioners who are not fans of the words process or governance, but the reality is that these do a lot to help provide structure to our human infallibility and help provide measures (commonly known as quality gates) that prevent aspects of good quality from making their way into production, and ultimately the users of our software.

That being said, humans by nature, are fickle and emotive beings. No structure that is too rigid by design is likely to be of benefit to a team and so with any of the approaches discussed in this chapter, there need to be aspects of flexibility built around which can allow our human natures to experiment, innovate, and learn along the way. After all, the opposite would make us robots and while AI has come a long way, there is too much complexity in designing fantastic software that can be reproduced by any form of repetitive process.

Quality is the responsibility of everyone
The key thing to remember though when building quality into your development process is to ensure that quality is the

responsibility of everyone on the team, all the way from product owner to designers and developers, along with the testers and shouldn't only be the primary focus of the latter.

Some of the responsibilities that the team members can follow include:

- Architects to design systems that are easily testable and modular in design – following the correct quality principles
- Business Analysts to define clear solutions for the teams to work towards, with a solid understanding of the underlying non-functional and technical requirements that make up a quality-driven software system.
- Developers to write clean, efficient, secure, maintainable, and performant code along with detailed unit tests
- Product Owners to assign the right amount of time for design, quality maintenance and testing development activities for all members of the team, but especially the core senior architects, dev, and testing leads.
- Managers to drive effective engagement and monitoring to motivate teams to achieve goals that consider the quality definitions that were established at the beginning of the book
- And lastly, testers to focus on testing at all levels and aid in developing core testing frameworks that can achieve the purpose of testing the software in an automated and efficient manner.

It is important to remember that software quality is as much a people problem as it is a technical one, so management needs to support processes that can not only drive quality development but create an environment that keeps people engaged and a part of the journey.

Think about quality from the start
The second key criterion is to get involved as early as possible. Which is one of the core reasons this book was written in the first place. So that systems can be designed with quality and software testing in mind and not be an afterthought in the development process.

This means that before we rush ahead and build any solution, we take the time out to properly understand the problem and rather see how we can build it with quality at the forefront of its design. This will take longer and feels expensive to companies that need to invest this time into work that seemingly looks like there is little output that comes from this approach – at least initially. If companies look at how the impact of poor quality affects other aspects of their bottom line, then they may be more willing to add an extra few weeks' worth of work to any project or delivery date to ensure that the team takes the time out to design it right the first time.

Quality requires a consistent approach
However, from my experience, the truth is that companies won't easily make this change and even when they start to place more emphasis on it, they will make mistakes along the way which might make them more hesitant about it.

Building quality processes

What is important though is fine-tuning the approach from all aspects to ensure all aspects of the software development process are continually aligned to the goal of quality development. Most often when I've seen companies fail in trying to implement quality design into their processes is when there is a gap between the expectations of design, development, or testing teams.

The same applies to different development or sprint teams themselves. Many companies want to build empowered teams that have the choice of how they build certain frameworks for their own products.
The problem is that this is wasteful, as it leads to duplication of effort as teams need to build frameworks that do the same thing; leads to poor quality as teams end up with different expectations of quality which will affect the output of other teams and prevents teams from learning from each other's mistakes.

And so, it's important that teams adhere to the same standard of quality, utilize the same test frameworks, and adhere to the same design and testing principles. This ensures that centralized tooling can better monitor quality across each product space.

It also makes the different software components integrate easier with each other, significantly reduces the integration testing effort, and prevents future errors, as shared learnings can be easily adopted across teams. It also has a further spin-off in that it is easier for people to move between teams as they will be familiar with the technologies and processes followed across teams.

Those who prefer teams to have certain levels of independence or autonomy need not be alarmed as teams can still have this, just within a bigger platform that will provide stability and predictability to the work the team does. Nott omentin other obvious gains to efficiency and quality that they will have because of these approaches.

Shift Left

Building quality into software requires a change from previous legacy test approaches which focused more on heavy testing later in a development cycle. While there was merit to this as it gave testing teams time to do thorough analysis while the developers were busy with the coding of a project. And yes, testers were still heavily involved in some of the early design and requirements phases of a project.

However, in keeping the majority of the testing approach too late in the project, major issues are only identified later that become far more expensive to fix, plus also may result in big architectural changes to fully address. Especially if these issues may relate to performance or security.

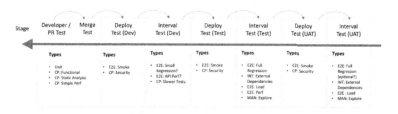

So, with a focus on designing for quality and testability coming up front, it needs to be backed by a focus on testing closer to the code and introducing a higher quality of testing across the whole stack. This means, from a testing perspective, a higher reliance on mocking to increase the testing coverage at these lower levels, but also requires a deeper understanding of how a system should work and allows the developers and testers the opportunity to ask the right questions to ensure they build their tests and mocks correctly.

And this includes performance and security testing, which are often reserved for very late in the development cycle. This is often because the system is not considered complete enough to warrant such scanning and testing. However, this is incorrect as testing even at a small component level, while appearing wasteful at times helps to correctly fine-tune and optimize the code.

Yes, it's true that fine-tuning small parts of code may not have much impact when used as an entire system in context, but the requirements that would lead to this are minimal and would be the exception rather than the norm, so it's still preferable to test this as early as possible.

Continuous Quality Improvement

Quality is not a destination. It needs continuous work and adaptation, and this is an important part of the quality process that can't be overlooked.

Any decent software development process needs to allow time for teams to revisit mistakes and come up with measures to address them and a proper root cause analysis process that evaluates the different reasons that may cause issues and satisfactorily addresses those root issues and not just the symptoms that surface because of them.

There are multiple approaches and ways of categorizing root causes of issues which are possibly endless depending on the context of different applications, though the below might be a good guideline for at least getting started.

When looking at analyzing issues in the development process, you want to look at three different things. Defect Types, Affected modules or components (where applicable), and then lastly a Root Cause. All of which I explain in more detail below:

Issue Types:
This is how an issue manifests itself in the code. While not all issues are necessarily code-related, the majority of the time we only notice them through defects in our software and so it's worth recording these.

- **Feature Defect** - this describes the fact that a new feature wasn't working, it manifests as new functionality not working as it should
- **Regression Defect** - this describes something that used to work, it manifests itself as functionality that used to work, and now doesn't
- **Performance Defect** - this describes the behavior of the system – its manifests as slow performance
- **Data Defect** - this describes something breaking for a specific piece of data – it's not broken for everything, but rather for specific data
- **System Outage** – this describes a defect that results in the system being down
- **Security Defect** – this describes a defect that is related to security. is manifests itself as a security breach in Production

- **Historic Defect** - this describes something that has been broken for a long time, this is something that isn't new – but it's only been discovered now
- **Known Defect** - this describes something that we knew was broken and was taken into production in a broken state, it's not something that manifests itself – it's something we KNEW about before deploying into our Production environment or is a duplicate of another known defect. Must link to a previous defect, otherwise, it's not known
- **Unknown** - Not yet classified. It's okay at the time of reporting any incident to not fully understand it yet, but this should only be a temporary measure and should be changed as the root cause of the issue is further established.

Modules Affected

Rather than being classified into any particular category, it's important that the underlying modules of code where defects occur are identified. This helps to track potentially problematic areas of code that can be looked at in more detail to perhaps either restructure the code or improve the level of testing around the underlying module.

Root Cause:

This is the core of what you want to identify through any issue. It's important as a team to dig through all the available data from the different monitoring systems and

- **Code Error – Code Quality** – Code change required to fix. There is an error in the code that needs to be changed to make it work as expected.

- **Code Error – Poor Design –** The issue lies with the overall architectural design and not just the specific code from the developer. While a code fix is required to rectify the problem, its underlying cause is related to the design of the system rather than a pure coding error on the part of the developer.
- **Data – Data Exception –** This was an outlying data sample that wasn't anticipated and caused an error. Data needs to be fixed.
- **Deployment – Library Corruption –** Library files got corrupted during the deployment process and the delivered code did not work as expected.
- **Deployment – Incorrect Build Script –** The incorrect code was deployed into production.
- **Deployment – Process Not Followed –** Team did not adhere to process in their deployment which led to the error.
- **Design - Missed Requirement –** Requirement was missed in the design process.
- **Design - Incorrect Requirement –** A requirement for this function exists but was incorrect.
- **Design - Impact Analysis Failure –** Team did not understand the impact this change had on other modules and dependencies and therefore did not cater to it in their development and testing.
- **Design - Missed Scenario -** The initial requirement was correct, but the team missed catering for this in testing.
- **Environment – Application Configuration –** The issue in production is a result of a configuration issue that needs to be changed.
- **Environment – System Failure –** There was an underlying fault in the hardware, Kubernetes or

other external systems that caused a failure with the code in production.

- **Environment – DB Issues –** The issue is the result of a failure with the database, DB process, or server itself.
- **Performance – Poor Code Optimization –** The performance issue is a result of a piece of non-DB-related code either on the front-end, BFF, or API layer.
- **Performance – DB Script Optimization –** The performance issue is a result of a poorly optimized SQL query.
- **Performance – Infrastructure –** Performance degradation is the result of the underlying hardware or system performance and is not code specific.
- **Not An Issue - Working as Expected –** Reported defect is actually the expected performance of the system as per requirement and will not be changed.
- **Not An Issue – User Error –** The issue is a result of user error and not any failure in the code or system.
- **Duplicate Issue –** The issue has been closed because it is a duplicate of another existing issue.
- **Tech Debt -** A known issue that the team was prepared to take into production and tackle in the future as Tech Debt.

As mentioned, this list is not extensive, but could also perhaps seem exhaustive and it's important that you as a company find a balance between categorizing issues in a way that gives you meaningful information

The focus of any improvement is on prevention rather than mitigation. And an issue is never truly solved until you as a team know how to prevent issues from occurring again. So, while the time looking into fixed issues at a deeper level might seem wasteful, it can add a lot of value to the future efficiency and quality delivery of a team. Especially when you consider the amount of time teams will typically spend supporting and fixing issues during any regular development cycle.

If done right, teams will learn from mistakes and develop ways of preventing certain issues from occurring and thereby focus on product delivery more efficiently and without distraction.

Quality Gates

A good testing process also takes into consideration the different levels of testing (which are discussed in a later chapter), how and where they need to be applied, who is responsible for this testing effort, and the measures that will be used to determine that this aspect of testing has passed.

This is where it becomes important to set up quality gates that can enforce the certain quality standards you want to send out and ensure that work does not continue on any part of the system until these quality gates have been met.

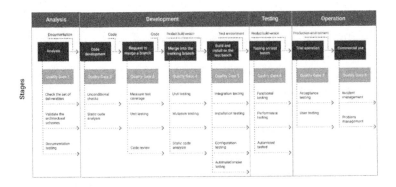

In a world focused on agile development, the notion of quality gates can often be frowned upon as it makes the test process look like more of a waterfall model than your typical agile approach. However, having a good quality gate structure shouldn't bring any change to whatever development approach is in use. All a quality gate does is ensure that teams don't go too far ahead of themselves without considering certain aspects of quality and prevent poor quality delivery from seeping into the later phases of the project. It encourages people to do the right thing and build quality into all the work that is done.

Even though I've presented an approach on the previous page, this may not mean it will work for every team or company. A good quality gate approach should include aspects of tracking the analysis of any piece of work and ensure measures are in place to ensure the team correctly understands what and how they are building something, using the agreed-upon architectural quality principles that a company has laid out.

Next would be building in various measures to evaluate the quality of the code and ensure developers are building the product right. Before it gets passed over to the testers and whatever further validation they may require. The measurement of the testing effort is important as it ensures code meets a certain standard before going into production and prevents teams from making risky decisions on whether to release or not, as the criteria should be firmly established that should make this decision as simple as possible.

For many companies though, quality gates may stop there, but they shouldn't. Quality gates should also look into the operation of an application and the different environments that keep any application going and we should ensure that we put certain gates in place to ensure that any module of code operates as expected at this level too.

Quality Gates help to provide structure to the quality efforts and ensure that standards are maintained across teams. How can you measure quality though? Well, for certain aspects of the development process - like an automated deployment pipeline – as shown in the approach suggested in the above picture, this can be a little more easily defined as we can use various tests and scans to identify and measure certain criteria around function, performance, or security test coverage.

The aspect that is perhaps more difficult to quantify is the early design phase which is most critical. What can be included here though is a thorough check against certain architectural principles set up for quality design and a review by a neutral team.

Predictability

Another key aspect of building a solid process and creating quality gates is that they create predictability in the development processes. As teams gain more familiarity with a quality approach and have an increase in quality output, the number of things that are likely to go wrong is reduced and this allows teams to become more reliable in their work.

Shared Responsibility and Accountability

This leads me to another very important part of any healthy quality process. The issue of dispersed responsibility and accountability. The truth is that no matter how great we might try and be as software engineers or architects, there will be aspects that others might be better equipped for and so it is important that we bring other skills into the mix to ensure that we broaden the expertise in the designing and review phases of a project.

This also creates accountability in that other people are also reviewing and verifying the process at all stages and is healthy for cross-skilling and creating a consistent process in an organization.

The trick here though is not broadening this too much as having too many people involved in the process could be wasteful and so you need to balance out the skills between the people that are most relevant and able to contribute, while also adding scope for training and development in the process too, to enable others to come up to speed. Typically, a power of three is considered good practice with an Architect, Tester, and Product Owner brought into the mix, though I would recommend increasing that to include a tech lead or other senior developer as well as a designer and a Scrum Master – to better align all parts of a team to what the team is trying to achieve.

This shared responsibility allows the team to collaborate on achieving quality together, better understand the needs of the other members of the team better, what it takes for each to deliver quality results, and importantly – bring accountability to all parties in achieving their quality deliverables.

Governance Matters

To ensure quality, there is no escaping the need for a good process and quality model that ensures teams are delivering on the required expectations and developing against the correct quality guidelines. So, even though process might be a bad word to many developers, don't shy away from it.

It's as important – or possibly even more important - to get the culture of your organization right to build a technical solution correctly.

Having a process in place is one thing, but what you want to avoid is just having a process in place for the sake of it and so to ensure your processes are working for you, it's important that we can measure them. Which is what we will discuss in the next chapter.

Building a Model for Quality Maturity

In the previous chapter, I spoke about the importance of building consistent processes to manage the quality of your software. It's more than just building a process though, but also being able to measure the effectiveness of the process and how well teams are adopting it.

Just because these best practices exist doesn't mean teams follow them and often bad habits and cultures can easily infiltrate teams that cause them to compromise on good quality practices. Leaving teams struggling to deliver the standard of software that they intended.

This is a difficult problem to solve. Especially for big companies with many cross-functional teams where it's difficult to retain core oversight in how they function. This is why things like Maturity Models exist. Allowing companies to provide some level of audit against software development teams to measure how well teams are adhering to certain practices and try and incentivize them to adopt them in scoring higher.

The idea behind Maturity Models is to provide some form of scoring or audit on how teams function. They list best practices that should be followed and then provide a measurement criterion to score how well teams are adopting these best practices. Allowing teams to maintain a level of autonomy and not provide a strictly enforced process that might not suit every team, but then at least provide an incentive on scoring them in how they're doing to encourage them to adopt and progress towards better quality practices.

The problem though with most maturity models is that they often go out of date very quickly, with best practices defined several years ago. Not always a good idea in working with some modern architectures and development processes. They can also be too theoretical and not practical enough, trying to focus on process adherence than actual results.

Secondly, having teams adhere to certain processes can simply create a tick-boxing exercise where teams end up just adding processes for the sake of it, without fully grasping its purpose, creating unnecessary admin, and slowing down their overall delivery as a result, with no actual quality gain.

Therefore, outside of companies measuring teams more effectively through a range of quality metrics internally, it's important for these maturity models to have some form of enforced metrics to better assess not just if teams are following the right processes, but actually delivering on them too.

And while there is no one size fits all solution here, I have tried to provide a model that can help teams include aspects of both process control and successful execution in adhering to it. It can be quite complicated to implement based on the tools utilized and the maturity of a company, but where these gaps exist, will hopefully encourage these teams to rethink these issues and start utilizing tools that better help them to measure these things.

Similarly, whereas some areas define measurement criteria

quite well, others are a little loosely defined. Largely because there may be vast differences in how they are measured across tools and different architectures. In these cases, I would encourage you to look to understand the core principles of what is trying to be measured in the metrics and see how it can be best achieved given a team's current tools and approach, without compromising on any of the core measurement criteria which are all important.

The core behaviors that you want to drive through a model like this are:

- Quality is the responsibility of every member of the team, and all should be playing their part in delivering high-quality software.
- Software testing should be automated as close to the code as possible, with a focus on unit testing.
- The appropriate automation coverage is achieved at different levels of the software
- Defects are tracked and resolved with the appropriate root causes identified
- Overall defect leakage is low for the team
- Performance and security measures are in place and showing results

To do this, a model assesses aspects of how a team collaborates on quality, the tooling in place, whether the reporting of quality is correct, and the overall processes followed with regards to testing and quality-related issues, along with some NFR specifics around performance and security.

Specific focus areas and metrics to be assessed across these measures include:

- Early involvement in testing
- Test Driven Development where tests are identified, and unit tests scripted before development has started
- Code Coverage for tests
- The prescribed testing framework and tools are being utilized
- Automation coverage across the appropriate levels (Unit, Component API, Front-end, Visual, End-to-end)
- Pipelines in places for all testing levels and pipeline execution time of adequately quality
- Security scanning in place - with a scoring to ensure teams adhere to it
- The appropriate performance testing is in place and executed at the correct level.
- Measurement of software performance against benchmarks
- Monitoring in place across both test environments and production
- Defect leakage rate (what the team misses in their sprints)
- Defect process (is the prescribed defect process adhered to with proper triage and RCA processes in place)
- Sprint retros are taking place with issues and mitigation places appropriate documented to drive improvement

Each of these aspects might seem insignificant on its own but does have an impact on the final quality delivered, either from a technical or cultural perspective. So, you want a model that can score these areas effectively.

There is no one way of doing this and there are many different approaches to modeling out there that look at different aspects of these criteria. Some focus on the technical side of things, others on the cultural – which is arguably very subjective and hard to measure.

I do try and suggest an approach below though that I have found to be quite useful in some projects I have worked on. It looks to measure technical aspects around the quality of testing coverage in an automated pipeline and provide guidance on performance and security while trying to provide some way of measuring adherence to quality best practices as well. Even though this latter point will still have an element of subjectivity to it.

How the Scoring Works

The below model scores the following areas that are then added together, to provide a score out of 700.
The seven scoring areas are:

- Code Coverage Scoring
- Pipeline Scoring
- E2E Test Coverage Scoring
- Process Scoring
- Defect Scoring
- Performance Scoring
- Security Scan Scoring

I have chosen these seven areas because I feel they cover a wide scope of quality deliverables. Assessing the strength of test scoring at different levels, the effectiveness of the CI pipeline process, performance, security, defect leakage, as well as some form of process adherence. WE could go into deeper levels of testing and score frameworks on how well they are written as well, but this becomes too complex, and the idea is to provide a model that can be easily implemented and understood without taking up too much overhead to maintain.

These scores will be collected from a combination of tooling to identify the coverage rates and defect calculations, along with a quarterly audit, where teams are scored on how well they are performing - with the incentive to improve their scores each time and face mitigation actions where scores are unsuitably low.

Code Coverage Scoring

Should be based on real code coverage for the application under test, across all measured tests. Whether it be unit tests, or lower-level automated component and integration tests. If they are automated and integrated into the build process, utilizing code coverage tools you should be able to calculate the percentage of code that has been touched by your tests.

By measuring this, you help to drive the creation of unit tests by your devs and ensure that more automated tests are integrated into the build process and not as something the testing team does separately.

There are many ways of calculating coverage. e common metrics that you might see mentioned in your coverage reports include:

- **Function coverage:** how many of the functions defined have been called.
- **Statement coverage:** how many of the statements in the program have been executed.
- **Branches coverage:** how many of the branches of the control structures (if statements for instance) have been executed.
- **Condition coverage:** how many of the boolean sub-expressions have been tested for a true and a false value.
- **Line coverage:** how many lines of source code have been tested.

These metrics are usually represented as the number of items tested, the items found in your code, and a coverage percentage (items tested / items found). Most coverage tools will provide a scoring for any of these metrics, but I would suggest trying to get a scoring for as many of these as possible and then divide it across the scores to get an average percentage out of 100.

Now, I'm not saying that scoring high on code coverage is a sign that testing has covered everything, but it does show that the team has put thought and effort into planning their testing and development. Whether that testing is correct should hopefully be caught at the E2E testing scoring level and will show in the defect scoring. You want to promote good test-driven development though and having a score that provides this is a critical way of doing that.

Pipeline Automation Scoring
This aspect of scoring might be less precise than code coverage, but the purpose of this is to ensure that a team is

integrating automated testing into the pipeline. You could argue that by measuring the code coverage score that this is being achieved in some way already but given that coverage scores can be added retrospectively and outside of a traditional build pipeline, it's important to also ensure that a healthy quality process is being followed and that the developer and testing team are both adding tests into a pipeline.

0 – No pipeline automation
20 – Unit & integration tests are running after merge to the main branch
40 - Unit & integration tests are running on every pull request
60 – E2E tests run after a merge to the main branch
80 – Integration tests validate dependent services before merging to the main branch
100 – Full e2e tests running before merging to the main branch

E2E Test Coverage Scoring
As mentioned in the code coverage section, high code coverage is not a guarantee that testing is either correct or that the integration points have been catered for, as these tests are often mocked. So, you also want to measure the end-to-end test coverage which will be conducted against an entire unmocked system.

However, as this coverage, even if automated and sitting in a pipeline, doesn't count against code coverage scores, you can't get as clear a scoring measurement. These tests may also often be done manually as they are not always feasible for automation due to their complexity.

What can be done though is that you can try, and score based on the coverage that has been covered by these end-to-end tests and give a rating based on that. Yes, this too is subjective and it's not always easy or wise to cover "all" scenarios, but as long as it provides a team with confidence in a type of testing, you can consider it covered and try and score as close to the below suggestions as possible.

0 – You do not verify the app is available
25 – You verify the app is available
50 – You verify the critical path scenarios
75 – You verify negative path scenarios
100 – You verify all paths scenarios

Process Scoring:
This is a measure of how well teams are adhering to certain testing processes. The processes identified here are good ones to have, but these will vary based on teams and culture and so should be adjusted to suit the needs of the company. Again, this is largely subjective, but still a good approach to build on.

Culture does not change overnight though and the nice thing with this scoring metric is that it helps to drive that change. You can encourage and incentivize teams to move closer to the correct process. Typically, what you would find is that teams that score low here are likely to score low elsewhere, so it provides some prescription into the culture changes required to help them not just score well here, but across the other scores too as well.

Quality by Design

The images that follow on the next page detail some of these behaviors that look at how well a team is collaborating, the type of tooling they are implementing, as well as the reporting and process approach in which they go about their testing and quality assurance.

	Maturity Model	Score
Initial - Building		0
Collaboration	Poor, ad-hoc communication, no training, little awareness of issues, individuals feel un heard when raising issues	
Tooling	No Tooling at all	
Reporting	Incident reports. Fire Fighting, users or third parties report incidents	
Process	Very reactive with little reproducible process to resolution	
Managed - Reactive, Manual		25
Collaboration	Testing is understood from a high level with general appreciation that something is needed but little understanding of what	
Tooling	Tools used externally from the programme and only external testing is undertaken	
Reporting	Reactive reports and emails around issues. No RCAs in place. Defect leakage and coverage not clear	
Process	QA maturity model initiated	
Defined - Analytics Led		50
Collaboration	Shared decision making and accountability around QA, NFRs, Agile and Dev-ops processes followed	
Tooling	Prescribed tooling in place, with some exceptions. API and front end scanning	
Reporting	Some near realtime dashboards for test environments. Test coverage and defect tracking in place	
Process	Working through the details of the Maturity Model and implementing changes to the programme to cover the lower performing areas of the programme	

Building a Model for Quality Maturity

Measured - Automated / CI - CD		75
Collaboration	Testing needs are considered at the start of sprints. Agile principles and retrospectives to identify inefficiencies in secure development	
Tooling	Prescribed tooling in place. Automated code scanning and reporting against API's and Frontend metrics captured	
Reporting	Realtime dashboards for all environments	
Process	Visibility and predictability of the entire process via the OWASP maturity model. Security metrics tracked from development into Production. RCA process for all defects	
Optimised - Driving Value / Automated		100
Collaboration	Knowledge sharing and empowerment. DevOps and Test-driven development in place	
Tooling	Self service, AI and machine learning via APM tooling	
Reporting	Full test coverage, performance and defect tracking in place. Real time alerts and bug creation directly linked to DevOps group to drive out solutions via sec ops and SRE	
Process	Optimization of Process, Risk and Cost	

Defect Scoring - Defect Leakage

While there is more to tracking defects than pure defect leakage, you can apply the below metric to assess the defect leakage score as it is a measure of what teams are missing in their project cycle. The reason for using a formula that calculates defects both before and after a defect release cycle as it should help to factor in the size and complexity of a release, so while bigger releases will likely have more defects post release, the team should have identified more as well, making the metric fairer.

CD=No. of Defects raised after release
DR=No. of Defects raised before release
ID- No. of invalid Defects from Defects raised before release (E.g., Duplicate, Cannot Fix, error in test environment etc.)
Formula to calculate Defect Leakage Defect Leakage= 100 - ((CD/(DR-ID))100).

We calculate the percentage of your defect leakage and then subtract that from 100 to provide a higher score for better performance. Should a defect leakage be over 100 percent, it

Quality by Design

should create a negative number which is added to the remaining scores and lowers the total maturity model score.

Performance Benchmarks
Once benchmarks have been clearly established, the performance of an application will be measured against the frequency of the performance runs along with the difference between the benchmark scores. The following metrics will form part of this benchmark measurement:

METRIC	DESCRIPTION
Conversations completed	The number of conversations that were completed during the selected timeframe.
Average response time	The average response time (time between each customer message and the next agent reply) of conversations that were completed within the filtered period.
Average resolution time	The average amount of time it took to complete conversations within the filtered period.
Messages received	The total number of posts received within the period. Click on the options below the graph to toggle channels.
Customer satisfaction score	The CSAT score calculated from completed conversations assigned to the agent or team within the filtered period.

All these scores should have a predetermined benchmark based on the needs of the functionality they support. The scores will then be determined based on the combined scores across all scenarios under test for the team:

Performance Results vs Benchmark	Score
10% deviation < Results	0
5% deviation < Results < 10% deviation	20
3% deviation < Results < 5% deviation	40
1.5% deviation < Results < 3% deviation	60
Benchmark < Results < 1.5% deviation	80
Results <= Benchmark	100

Security Scans

Software scans need to be run against the code to ensure that security best practices are adhered to and that known vulnerabilities have been mitigated. Scoring for this depends on the chosen tools to measure the security of the code, though given the popularity of tools like Black Duck/Checkmark which apart from just raising security risks to the development team, also provides a scoring system out of 10 (or 100), which will be used to measure how a team scores in this area. Note though, that security scan scores can easily be improved by removing scanning from certain modules, so the metrics will only count against the scanning of all developed code:

Scoring

Tool score out of 10: **Security Scan score** = security tool score from 100% coverage * 10

Tool score out of 100: **Security Scan score** = security tool score from 100% coverage

In the absence of a scoring system, you can leverage a percentage of failures versus the lines of code as a score to measure. Much like some of the other scores, its less about being precise and rather trying to drive the right behaviors. So, even if you have to score this a little subjectively, it can still create the right awareness and help to reduce the errors in your security efforts, however, they are scanned or measured.

Visibility drives accountability and change

This might all sound like a complex set of calculations and measurements that need to be maintained. Especially with companies that have a high number of teams. However, most of these measures can be easily tracked through tooling and made visible to teams live with only the basic process audit requiring a deliberate manual effort to score – and even this can be tracked through the evidence provided by certain process management or sprint tools to make things even easier. Ultimately, you can still remove this measure as well if you feel these other scores will help drive the right testing behaviors.

It would be great to not need a maturity model. Especially in this DevOps world where most of the quality should be controlled in a coding pipeline. However, the reality is that many teams find themselves in very different spaces depending on their history, architecture, and purpose and so a maturity model is a way of helping teams move in the right direction without restricting their ability to still be productive.

Building the right quality gates into your CI pipeline

Continuous Integration is the aim of many development teams wanting to quickly add new features and make changes to their software and deliver them to production as fast as possible. Doing so while maintaining a good view of quality though is something that is far more difficult to get right. And a lot of this is because teams might be quick to adopt a CI pipeline, but they are not willing to implement the right measures or quality gates into the process that will ensure the software is of high quality.

Many of the reasons for this range from a lack of sufficient skills in a team, especially at a testing level where the team is not able to automate the appropriate level of testing where it is needed, a lack of understanding of what needs to be done – or often and most importantly, - lack of time to truly implement measures that will make this work, as teams focus on the delivery of software rather than investing time in quality best practices.

As mentioned in the chapter on Building Quality Processes, Quality Gates are steps in your Software Development Process that will help teams determine if their project and software are in a suitable place before continuing further. It allows teams to build quality processes early and not move too far along in the development process without certain protocols in place, as these would be more expensive to implement later.

However, most software engineers are not massive fans of process and audit checks. Even if they're incredibly valuable. This is why a good way of building quality processes into a team is via the pipeline. Most teams understand the value of a build pipeline and the need to put a level of tests in the process to prevent things from breaking. With many teams not making the full value of the testing process at a pipeline level though, this also becomes a pivotal way to be able to ensure that the right level of testing is done, in a way that is not overly "regulated" through a process but automated directly into their code deployment. Essentially, allowing you to gain the benefits of proper quality control, in a way that is automated and easily digestible to the development team

Building quality gated into a pipeline is unfortunately a battle that often gets lost on the quality front as other things take priority over the needed investment in skills and measures to produce high-quality software. Though if you are in a position to start a new pipeline governance system from scratch and need some assistance in knowing what is needed to make an effective high-quality pipeline, well then, the below guidelines should help you.

While not every aspect of the pipeline quality measures is critical, they certainly all add significant value and so if for whatever reason a team has decided to skip them, is important that a team understand these risks and puts in mitigation to check for this elsewhere.

The below pipeline outline should also apply regardless of whether your systems are hosted internally or on the cloud, though I do understand the complexities and costs involved in having complex test environments that match production.

In my opinion, though, the costs are worth it. The benefit gained from improved quality and reduced maintenance on your development budget cannot be overstated enough. Though if you have a system that is completely built around Infrastructure as Code, then it is possible to get by without a permanent environment and use just a scaling one – as this is what production would imitate anyway.

Structure of CI Pipeline

Below is an image where I provide an example of an automated pipeline with the relevant quality gates in it. I will go into detail describing the different phases of the pipeline and the checks involved to help build quality into the process. I do understand that this is a very simplistic pipeline example and no doubt your needs may be different and possibly more complex.

The idea though is to provide a guideline of important checks that should be instituted and for you and your teams to take it upon yourselves to find out how best to implement them into your own development pipelines.

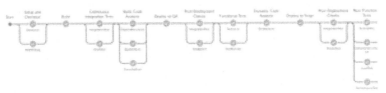

The purpose of having our CI pipelines structured like this is to ensure that there is a check at every level to verify the correctness of the code, build, and deployment. Each step is described in more detail below:

Setup and Checkout
The developer checks out the code. A setup file should be present to ensure that the environment is then built to be consistent for each developer, as they follow the correct standards. Part of this setup includes several linting standards that will also check that certain coding principles are been adhered to and will prevent code from being deployed where it does not meet these appropriate linting standards.

Quality Check: Linting standards need to be met before code build can be successful.

Build
Once a developer is ready to submit their code, the pipeline will take their code and build it in a container/mocked environment which will form the basis of the unit tests.

Unit tests/CI Tests
These tests include both the unit tests written by the developer for the modules under development and some broader component tests which will represent the execution across all the modules, but at a mocked level.

Quality Check: 100% successful completion of all tests with a 90% code coverage achieved at a unit testing level.

Static Analysis
The relevant static analysis scans and security scans are run against the code base to ensure that certain coding and security best practices have been adhered to.

Quality Check: Successful completion of scans with 100% code coverage.

Deployment to QA
It is only at this point that the code is deployed into an integrated test environment where it will exist against other unmocked modules that will run tests developed by the testing team to cover a wider range of unmocked integration tests and end-to-end tests. This environment can be scaled up and down based on the testing needs and does not need to live all the time. This environment will also form a wholly usable state of the system with only minimal mocking in place to allow the team to do a few manual verification checks should they be needed.

Post-Deployment Checks
These are contract-level tests that will run to ensure that the test environment meets the required expectations of the deployment code and some lightweight tests of the code to ensure that it is working effectively within the test environment. Should it fail here, the code is rolled back, and the QA environment restored.

Quality Check: Successful passing of all post-deployment and smoke tests.

Functional Tests
This is where the remainder of the automated tests identified by the testing team are executed, which will span a wider coverage of the codebase and include some unmocked tests as well, with more realistic data that better resembles that of production.

Quality Check: All tests need to be passed.

Dynamic Code Analysis

This is another scan that is run against executable code (unlike the static analysis scans which are run against pre-deployed code) and provides an additional measure of quality and security checks like SQL queries, Long input strings (to exploit buffer overflow vulnerabilities), Negative and large positive numbers (to detect integer overflow and underflow vulnerabilities) and unexpected input data (to exploit invalid assumptions by developers). These are all vital checks that are best run against an actual working environment.

Quality Check: Successful completion of scans.

Deploy to staging

The code is then passed on to a staging environment, which is another integrated environment, but one that better reflects the state of production. Also, unlike test environments which can be scaled up and down, this one should be permanently available and configured as the code would be in production. Any final manual or automated validations from the testing team can also be conducted at this time by the testing team, though won't necessarily form part of the automated tests unless the testing team deems it necessary.

Post-Deployment Checks

As was conducted against the QA environment, a set of post-deployment tests are run to ensure that the staging environment is in the correct state and smoke tests are executed to ensure the deployed code is in a usable state.

Quality Check: Successful passing of all post-deployment and smoke tests.

Non-functional Test execution
It's at this stage that all load, performance, and additional security tests are executed to ensure that the code meets all the required NFR standards before being deployed into production.

Quality Check: Successful completion and passing of all NFR tests.

It is only at this stage that the code is deemed sufficient to be deployed to production.

There is obviously a lot more detail in making a pipeline like this work, especially in ensuring that the right testing skills and tools are in place, but if a team can develop a framework that measures all these aspects and the team endeavors to meet them, regardless of how strict, then a team should easily be capable of producing mostly error-free software to prediction in a rapid manner.

Conclusion

Hopefully, it's been made clear to you as you've worked through this book that software quality involves more than we realize and requires plenty of deliberate and careful thought to get right.

It's vital that we approach the design of our software carefully to ensure we are building systems with the appropriate architectures that meet the functional, maintainable, security, and performance needs that are required in a modern-day software system. And all this before we've even factored in our testing approach.

These are not things that we can turn around overnight and often many of us land up in situations where we feel we may not be able to influence this change to designing a quality system. Every minor change makes a difference though and even if you focus on ensuring that all the work you do moves towards building and testing software in a quality context, then you help trigger the culture change that is needed.

Stay humble and keep learning

There is no such thing as a perfect system and there are always likely to be things we can learn from and improve over time to better enhance software quality. So, be prepared to keep learning to find better ways of doing things, while acknowledging that there are other approaches out there that may work just as well, or possibly even better.

Conclusion

It's also important to keep learning and growing with the technological changes and there is no doubt that new solutions, tools, and approaches will come along that may drastically help improve aspects of how we design software for the better. As an industry professional, you want to keep learning to be on top of these new ideas and approaches so that you can apply and implement them as soon as possible.

Even if I classify myself as a quality expert, I know that there are many branches of software development and frameworks and tools that I am not familiar with and there are regular new approaches that I come along and realize work better than solutions I would've tried. So, don't ever think that you have learned everything and rather approach every problem with the goal of learning. This will help you to make the best decisions for your team and company and not only lead the company to designing better software, but you are having a more developed skillset too.

Be a part of the solution

We can all play a part in bringing about change in the organizations and software we work with. Most people don't react to change well, and large change can easily trip up the best teams. So, as you work on improving the quality of software wherever you are, take your time to properly learn the systems, understand the problem space and focus on the biggest areas where change is required.

The best way we can bring about change is by supporting a team and building the strength within their current design and processes and introducing change slowly and methodically.

Be a part of the future

And it is not just about changing software to be of better quality but ensuring that the software we build today meets the needs of tomorrow. So, the effort we put in today to work on designing and building better software systems will help ensure both your skillset and the software you are working on can outlive the effort you have put into it.

And building software that remains reliable, performant, and helps build the companies we work for into big success, is part of a legacy we want to contribute to and be a part of.

Good luck on this journey and although it won't be an easy one, I hope you can make a big impact in building software that is of high quality and make a difference in a software-driven world that needs software that is built right.

Printed in Great Britain
by Amazon

32170452R00188